Treasured

Praise for
Treasured

"In *Treasured,* Leigh McLeroy invites the reader to join her quest to know God's heart for His child. Well written, winsome, and fearlessly honest, this is a reassuring read for the soul who hungers for God's love."

> —CAROLYN CUSTIS JAMES, author of *The Gospel of Ruth:*
> *Loving God Enough to Break the Rules*

"What a refreshing and surprising book! Until I read *Treasured,* I never considered how a few easily overlooked things in Scripture could have such power to help us know God more truly and intimately. With delightful prose and biblically shaped wisdom, Leigh McLeroy leads us into a deeper encounter with our living, loving God."

> —DR. MARK D. ROBERTS, senior director
> and scholar-in-residence for Laity Lodge

"I enjoyed watching [Leigh McLeroy] deftly polish the treasures God might keep in His memory box. She helped me notice God's engagement with us. If God feels distant to you, *Treasured* will imaginatively and biblically illustrate His tenderness."

> —JONALYN GRACE FINCHER, national speaker with
> Soulation (www.soulation.org) and author of *Ruby*
> *Slippers: How the Soul of a Woman Brings Her Home*

"Leigh McLeroy has interwoven her story with God's story—a rich tale of treasures and being treasured. She has done what I love in good writing: mixed sweet memories, profound observations, sharp insights, and exquisite words into a delicious narrative."

—JUDY DOUGLASS, director of Women's Resources, Campus Crusade for Christ, and cofounder of Synergy Women's Network

Treasured

Treasured

Knowing God
by the Things
He Keeps

Leigh McLeroy

WATERBROOK
PRESS

TREASURED
PUBLISHED BY WATERBROOK PRESS
12265 Oracle Boulevard, Suite 200
Colorado Springs, Colorado 80921

ISBN 978-1-4000-7481-5
ISBN 978-0-307-45832-2 (electronic)

Copyright © 2009 by Leigh McLeroy

Published in association with the literary agency of Alive Communications Inc., 7680 Goddard Street,
Suite 200, Colorado Springs, CO 80920, www.alivecommunications.com.

Published in the United States by WaterBrook Multnomah, an imprint of the Crown Publishing Group,
a division of Random House Inc., New York.

WATERBROOK and its deer colophon are registered trademarks of Random House Inc.

Library of Congress Cataloging-in-Publication Data
McLeroy, Leigh
  Treasured : knowing God by the things He keeps / Leigh McLeroy. — 1st ed.
    p. cm.
  Includes bibliographical references.
  ISBN 978-1-4000-7481-5 — ISBN 978-0-307-45832-2 (electronic)
  1. Spirituality. 2. Christian antiquities. 3. Bible—Antiquities. 4. Signs and symbols. 5. Autobiography—
Religious aspects—Christianity. 6. Storytelling—Religious aspects—Christianity. I. Title.
  BV4501.3.M3736 2009
  231—dc22

                    2009011123

Printed in the United States of America
2009—First Edition

10 9 8 7 6 5 4 3 2 1

SPECIAL SALES
Most WaterBrook Multnomah books are available at special quantity discounts when purchased in bulk
by corporations, organizations, and special-interest groups. Custom imprinting or excerpting can also be
done to fit special needs. For information, please e-mail SpecialMarkets@WaterBrookMultnomah.com
or call 1-800-603-7051.

In loving memory of:

Alice Elizabeth Nixon Smith
Willis Bryant Smith
Frances Winona Hawthorne McLeroy
Walter Buford McLeroy Sr.
(I knew them as Memaw, Pepaw, Grand Nona, and Daddy Mac.)

Contents

Introduction: My Grandfather's Box 1
Memories by Mail

1 A Fig Leaf 7
The God Who Covers Me

2 A Fresh Olive Sprig 21
The God of New Beginnings

3 A Dry Waterskin 35
The God Who Sees

4 Abraham's Knife 49
The God Who Provides

5 A Strip of Bloodied Cloth 63
The God with a Bigger Plan

6 A Bloodstained Piece of Wood 77
The God Who Defeats Death

7 A Golden Bell 91
The God of Show and Tell

8   A Scarlet Cord 105
The God Who Includes

9   Balaam's Riding Crop 119
The God Who Speaks

10   A Head of Barley 135
The God Who Gleans Joy from Sorrow

11   A Shepherd's Harp String 149
The God of the Little Guy

12   One Smooth Stone 161
The God Who Writes on Hearts

13   Inside My Cigar Box 169
The Things That Make the Story Mine

End Note: What's in Your Box? 191
Personal Reflection and Group Discussion Guide

Acknowledgments 201

Notes 203

My Grandfather's Box

Memories by Mail

A battered cardboard box arrived by mail a few weeks after my grandfather's death, postmarked from the small West Texas town where he lived most of his years, the town where a crumbling cemetery now cradled his remains.

Inside the box, suspended in weightless drifts of white Styrofoam, a smaller, more pungent box was buried. An old cigar box.

Like young Jem Finch of *To Kill a Mockingbird,* I lifted the lid of my newly arrived treasure chest in private. But instead of carved soap figures, marbles, and other childhood collectibles, I saw a handwritten note: "Here are some of Pepaw's things." Then, in an obvious afterthought: "He kept these."

The well-meaning aunt who sent this shipment must have intended to place some final mark of punctuation on my grandfather's interrupted ninth decade, but for his youngest daughter's youngest daughter, the box formed not a period but a colon. *Meet your grandfather,* it seemed to say. *Maybe you didn't know him so well after all.*

If I had expected some sort of inventoried order, I would have been disappointed. It looked as if Willis Smith had simply emptied his pockets on his last day, filling the cigar box with the contents of his neatly creased khakis, as if to say, *There you go. That 'bout does it.*

I lowered my face and inhaled deeply, breathing in the last, elusive fragrance of a man I had adored. Nothing in the box could have been worth more than a few dollars, and there was not a single keepsake that might be considered suitable for display. But every small scrap it contained told a story—his story.

A stiff-bristled shaving brush sported a worn wooden handle with lettering that had long ago faded into hieroglyphics. I held it with thumb and forefinger and stroked it down my jawbone from cheek to chin. It still smelled faintly sweet. Willis's face was always clean-shaven and splashed liberally with Old Spice. He was an outdoor man who cleaned up well and wore his hat to town.

Near the brush was a polished nickel lighter—its top hinged back with a click, releasing the tinny aroma of lighter fluid. I tried to ignite a flame, brushing the striker wheel smartly with my thumb, but there was no juice left, not even the tiniest glimmer of a spark.

Next, I fingered a small leather coin purse with a doll-sized zipper. It contained a little more than a dollar in loose change. Cradling the coins in my palm, I imagined my grandfather standing with them at the cash register in Keel Drug Store and buying…what? A roll of butterscotch disks? A package of Swisher Sweets? I wasn't sure. But at Keel's they would know, because nearly every day for at least twenty-five years, he had ambled in there for a sandwich, a prescription, or a few minutes of friendly speculation about the size of the current maize crop, or the weather, or both.

His battered brown wallet with a single fold contained no driver's license (failing eyesight meant he hadn't driven legally for years), but it yielded up a Social Security card that looked newer than my own, along with a Medicare ID and a printed business card—mine, from my first job out of college. He hadn't said a word when I shyly handed it to him, but he apparently deemed it important enough to keep. I remembered him introducing me once to a crony of his with this preamble: "This is my daughter Muriel's youngest girl. She's an old maid." I was twenty-one at the time. But maybe he hadn't been so disappointed in me after all.

Next to the wallet were two identical, palm-sized Bible promise books filled with predictable but encouraging words from the King James Version: "The LORD is my shepherd; I shall not want" (Psalm 23:1). And, "That whosoever believeth in him should not perish, but have everlasting life" (John 3:16). I had never once seen Willis read the Bible, never gone with him to church. I imagined the tiny books propped up on his meal tray at the nursing home, maybe as a special gift to residents on Easter or Christmas. Did he finally help himself to the great "whosoever" invitation of God?

I never knew for certain. One day I will.

Two matching cuff links and a tie tack told me that my grandfather had dressed at least once for something more formal than an afternoon at the domino hall, although I couldn't imagine what. A court date? A friend's funeral? At my high-school graduation he wore a neatly pressed dress shirt with the top button buttoned…but no tie. That was as gussied up as I had ever seen him.

Last, I fingered a single key ring with two keys. To what? What did he open in the end that he might have locked? He'd experienced the indignity of aging, the sort of dependency that invites access. After a while everyone comes in, and hardly anyone knocks. Independence becomes a distant memory, privacy a mirage. But to his dying day my grandfather apparently carried keys…even if they hadn't opened anything in years.

As I held the contents of that box in my lap, I felt grateful, and powerfully connected—not just to the Willis I knew, but to the life that was his before I was born, and to the angles and edges of him that I had never seen with my own eyes. He came alive for me through the contents of one small box in a way he never had before, with his mystery, his sweetness, and his scars. Now he would exist for me not in flesh and bone but through the tangible scraps of memory he left behind, things that painted for me a fresh, new picture of the man.

I've known God longer than I ever knew my grandfather, although I have never seen Him. I've not once touched His face or heard His voice or felt the weight of His hand on my own. Still, I suspect that He has left more than a few scattered bits of His rich and mysterious identity for me to examine, tucked away deep in the pages of His Word. An olive branch here. A golden bell there. A faded strip of fabric, spotted brown with blood. A length of scarlet thread. A few grains of barley. These keepsakes tell His story, and they help me to understand my own.

He treasured them, and He treasures me too.

A Fig Leaf

The God Who Covers Me

When the woman saw that the tree was good for food, and that it was a delight to the eyes, and that the tree was desirable to make one wise, she took from its fruit and ate; and she gave also to her husband with her, and he ate. Then the eyes of both of them were opened, and they knew that they were naked; and they sewed fig leaves together and made themselves loin coverings.

—Genesis 3:6–7

The leaf is very nearly palm sized, a broad, trefoil shape—and a kind of rough fuzz covers both its top and its underside. It doesn't seem a texture that would rest comfortably next to human skin. However, it is easily plucked from the fig tree's branches, and fairly sturdy, I suppose, for garden wear. When trying to cover up quickly, we reach for what is closest, so for Adam and Eve, this must have been a most convenient cover-up.

I heard her before I saw her: a hoarse, loud woman who barked awful obscenities at no one in particular. On a bench near New York's old Plaza Hotel, a friend and I had paused to fortify ourselves with coffee and street-vendor bagels before more sightseeing. As our eyes scanned in the direction of the voice, we spied its source: a disheveled, clearly agitated woman carrying an odd assortment of plastic bags and a battered cane. She now veered in our direction.

"Look down," my friend instructed quietly. "Don't look at her."

I was twenty-three years old. It was my first trip to the city. I couldn't help but look at her. I'd never seen a sight quite like her before. Then the randomly screeching woman aimed her moving tirade like a laser…at the two of us.

"Look at yourselves," she screamed, coming closer. "Just look at yourselves. You make me sick. You make me sick. Shame! Shame!"

She came so close that I finally did look down, but only to avoid being hit by the spittle flying from her mouth as she berated us.

"You should be ashamed," she barked. "You make me sick!" Then, as abruptly as she had zeroed in on us, she began moving across the small park area in the direction of a retreating homeless man not twenty yards away.

I looked at my friend wide-eyed, unsure whether to laugh or cry. As bizarre as the experience had been, the woman who verbally accosted us that chilly day in Manhattan was not saying anything I hadn't heard before…from deep within my own heart. My inner critic isn't dramatically loud and doesn't spit, but she can be just as condemning, and her out-of-the-blue rants equally mean and focused. *And you call yourself a Christian,* she rails, or, *They just invited you to be polite,* or, *Shut up before you embarrass yourself. Everyone can tell you don't know what you're talking about.*

Sometimes when I look at myself, I get upset at what I see and am more than a little ashamed. I know my own shortcomings better than anyone. I can point them out almost without thinking, like a tour guide who's frequented the same spots for so long she doesn't even have to engage her brain to rattle off the particulars. "Yes, over here we have stubborn pride… It's been here since the beginning. And over here is envy, and over there greed. We may see some sloth today if the weather's nice…and perhaps a bit of gluttony too."

It doesn't take an unfortunate woman off her meds to convince me I've got issues. I know that I do. Parts of me are just as sick and shame filled as she insisted that day, only my infirmities are better hidden than her own.

G. K. Chesterton once said that original sin was the one Christian doctrine he could not challenge, for he had personal, empirical evidence of its veracity.[1]

Once upon a brief but beautiful sliver of time, shame did not exist. It simply wasn't. In the ancient, God-planted garden we know as Eden, the first man and the first woman lived without it. Adam and Eve really were made for each other, and never would there be a more promising beginning than theirs. It was just the two of them, ensconced in a lush paradise where "the LORD God caused to grow every tree that is pleasing to the sight and good for food; the tree of life also in the midst of the garden, and the tree of the knowledge of good and evil" (Genesis 2:9).

In this paradise, two totally unique but perfectly interdependent persons lived as one flesh. "And the man and his wife were both naked," the story goes, "and were not ashamed" (2:25). Adam felt no drawing back from Eve. All of him was open, visible, and knowable to her. And all of her to him. No inner sentry warned them to protect themselves from each other or even hinted that they were vulnerable to hurt. They each had a baby's innocence, having never been babies at all.

There was work to be done in Eden. Cultivating and keeping work. Tending work. Stewardship. And there were rules. To Adam, the Lord God commanded: "From any tree of the garden you may eat freely; but from the tree of the knowledge of good and evil you shall not eat, for in the day that you eat from it you will surely die" (2:16–17). He gave Adam this instruction even before He gave him Eve. But it wasn't long before things went badly awry.

"Now the serpent," we are told, "was more crafty than any beast of the field which the LORD God had made. And he said to the woman, 'Indeed, has God said, "You shall not eat from any tree of the garden"?' The woman said to the serpent, 'From the fruit of the trees of the garden we may eat; but from the fruit of the tree which is in the middle of the garden, God has said, "You shall not eat from it or touch it, or you will die" '" (3:1–3).

In Eve's own words, the serpent quickly recognized his in. She had identified something that God said was off-limits to her. He could convince her that God's commands concerning the tree in the center of the garden were grossly unfair, that her Creator really did not have her best interests at heart—but meant to withhold from her something very good. He could fool her into believing that God's prescribed limits kept her from true fulfillment. (In all this time his story has not changed one iota.) He further disputed that God's predicted consequences were true: "You surely will not die!" he told her. "For God knows that in the day you eat from it your eyes will be opened, and you will be like God, knowing good and evil" (3:4–5).

But too much of the wrong kind of enlightenment is never a good thing.

Convinced of the forbidden tree's desirability (and of God's aloofness toward her now-clamoring wants), Eve ate. And she invited Adam to join her. He may or may not have been privy to the serpent's wooing of Eve, but he had surely heard firsthand God's command to abstain. He ate anyway, with cosmic repercussions: "Then the eyes of both of them were opened, and they knew that they were naked, and they sewed fig leaves together and made themselves loin coverings" (3:7).

The new knowing that Adam and Eve's disobedience brought

to them was no comfort, but instead a curse. For the first time, they saw before them not God's beauty but their own flawed hearts. They felt guilty as a result of their sin, and that guilt made them want to hide—from God and from each other. So they took fig leaves (scratchy, broad, trefoil-shaped patches) and sewed them together to cover themselves as best they could. But even covered, they still felt shame.

The promised damage of sin had begun.

"Shame," says John Piper, "is the painful emotion caused by a consciousness of guilt or shortcoming or impropriety."[2]

Some shame is justified or well placed; some is not. But once sin comes into the picture, shame is sure to follow. We come to understand why God says no most clearly when we have disobeyed Him and begin to feel the weight of the consequences our actions bring. Sooner or later, with sin comes shame. They are close companions. One rarely shows up without the other. One invites the other to the party: Shame…and guest. Sin…and guest. Shame just may be the most debilitating chronic disease known to man. It makes us heartsick at the sight of ourselves. It makes us want to cover our shortcomings from other people's sight. And it puts distance between us and those we would love—and those who would love us.

Shame is like a lumbering dog that creeps uninvited into bed and insinuates itself between bedmates, then proceeds to claim the space between them as no man's land so that they can never touch, never hold each other, never speak without reaching over or past something big and rank and formidable.

I know this dog better than I wish I did.

I think I might have grown up wanting to hide. I can remember routinely making a tent of my bedcovers with a twirling baton for a center pole and crawling underneath it for cover. I played there with my dolls and storybooks. I liked it under the tent. About the same time—when I was a first grader—I was unwillingly segregated from the rest of the classroom for hours at a time when my teacher discovered I could read. I had learned easily alongside my older sister two years earlier. When she brought home beginner books, I watched over her shoulder as she sounded out the words. Soon I was poring over them alone, piecing the stories together as she did and loving every minute of it. But a reader in a classroom of nonreaders was an inconvenience for my teacher, and so she dragged my desk over to a corner and piled a stack of library books nearby to keep me occupied. I must have mentioned to my parents that I was sad being alone so much of the day, which necessitated a rather uncomfortable parent-teacher conference. My mother told me years later that my dad nearly leaped over the principal's desk and grabbed him by the throat when he informed my parents that "no first grader should be that d—— smart." I didn't feel like an overachiever, though; I felt like a freak.

I was in third grade when another teacher discovered that I could write poetry (once a word nerd, always a word nerd) and horrified me by filling a glass trophy case in front of the main office with huge copies of poems I'd done for class, illustrated on poster board for all the school to see. If I could have carried my homemade tent with me as a portable hiding place after that, I believe I would have. The coolest kids in class were fast runners on the playground or social magnets for clusters of other kids at the lunch table; I was the trophy-case poet. I felt even odder than I probably was.

No one had to teach me to be ashamed of being different. It came naturally. I didn't trust anyone to "get" me, and I wasn't exactly brimming with confidence over whatever early talent I might have demonstrated. Like any other kid, I just wanted to fit in. At home I knew I was loved, but open, easy praise wasn't often offered or encouraged.

Once, a favorite aunt was brushing my long, thick ponytail while we sat in her living room watching the Miss America Pageant. "You're so pretty," she told me as she pulled the brush through my hair. "You're prettier than all those girls there on the television." I felt my heart open wide. I wanted so much to believe her that for a brief moment I did. My mother overheard her compliment, though, and—I'm sure to make certain her already slightly precocious preteen daughter didn't get bigheaded—quickly corrected her: "No, she's not. Don't tell her that."

I wanted to sink into the sofa cushions for my half second of willing belief. Of course it wasn't true. I was ashamed that I had thought it might be. I wasn't even ten, and I was already toting around loads of misplaced shame. Score one for Satan, with an easy assist from my ancestor Eve.

When Adam and Eve realized their physical and emotional nakedness, their misplaced shame bound them too. Their natural trust in each other gave way to suspicion. They interacted carefully instead of with carefree ease. The pure, intimate bond between them became shadowed by cautious restraint. Since their fall, self-protection, not transparency, has been our human bent.

When I got a little older, I experienced well-placed shame. My own moral compass let me know when I was out of bounds, and it routinely set off shame alarms. As with Adam and Eve, I'd had the rules for right living clearly articulated to me. I knew my parents' expectations. And I knew when I had defied and disappointed them.

Unfounded or well placed, this remnant of shame has been consistently present all my life—as either a low-grade feeling of unease or a sharp sense of remorse, regret, and longing for cover. I still grapple with it. Like Adam and Eve, I try to close the gap between what *is* and what *ought to be* by covering what *is*. But my covering is never quite adequate. It keeps slipping off at the most unexpected times.

꧁

My task was simple: pick up the morning paper and a carton of juice. *Easy in, easy out.* Five minutes max. I strode with purpose into my neighborhood grocery store, grabbed the juice, swiped a paper off the stack, and queued up in the express line behind three other sleepy-eyed customers—none of whom, I noted gratefully, had more than ten items.

But the line wasn't moving. I shifted from one foot to the other as the young cashier chatted up her customers, taking her sweet time and even commenting with great interest on their purchases: "Oh, I love cherries! I didn't see these—they look really good." And, "I've never tried this detergent before. Do you like it?" By the time she got to my two items, I was nearing meltdown. When she scanned the carton of juice and the *Chronicle* without hesitating, I thought we might be getting somewhere. But once that was done, she placed my paper squarely in front of her, stared at the headlines, and began reading them to me. Out loud. Slowly and with great interest. " 'Rains cause local flooding. Inmate escapes from county jail.' Did you see this?"

I hadn't. But I'd hoped to. At home. With a glass of juice. *For myself.*

"No," I said, "I didn't. And I'd really like to read it *first,* if you don't mind."

Her sweet face fell. Her smile disappeared. Although I instantly felt guilty for being so rude, I was sure she was about to apologize for dawdling—and for previewing my paper. After all, I had tried to shame her with my words. But she didn't apologize. She looked at me with great concern and said, "You must be having a really bad day."

Oh yes, I was. In more ways than one. She wasn't checking my groceries inaccurately, and she did not have a bad attitude. She wasn't lazy or rude or cranky. She was just slow. And friendly. I was dead wrong, and I knew it. Shame fell over me like a curtain weighted at the hem. My first thought was of how rude I had been to her. My second was, *I hope she doesn't know me from church.*

In that moment I was reminded of a story I'd heard about the late Rich Mullins, traveling in Amsterdam with his buddy Beaker. The two of them were in a train station, talking about the temptations they had encountered in the freewheeling city and how they'd struggled with resisting them. Just then, a man sitting nearby turned to Rich and said, "You're Rich Mullins, aren't you?" Rich's response was, "It depends. What did you just hear?"

God did not leave Adam and Eve for long in their flimsy fig-leaf wardrobe. After He called out to them and they confessed, He made them more durable garments of animal skin and clothed them Himself. His covering confirmed that there *was* something to their shame, and it bore witness to the innocence they had, in fact, lost. He agreed with them that they now needed covering. But He insisted on doing it Himself, rejecting their self-covering and replacing it with a superior one of His own design. Later He would permanently solve the problem of their shame (along with yours and mine) with the blood of His own Son, clothing His children instead with the righteousness of Christ and the radiance of His resurrected glory.

Like my ancestors, I have my own do-it-yourself shame cover-ups. Words are useful in this regard—especially if you have an apt facility with them. They're one of my favorite coverings. Like Adam and Eve, I can carefully layer whatever might be close at hand to cover the fact that I see myself as I am but want the rest of the world to see me as I'd like to be. Piousness can be a cover-up. Doing right. Being right. Living right. These are my fig leaves…but they're never enough. Not enough to justify my sinful nature or even to hide from myself the fact that I'm fatally flawed. At the end of the day, none of my ad hoc fig leaves work.

Much has been made of the fact that God replaced Adam and Eve's make-do foliage with animal skins, that this was the Bible's first bloodshed—a foreshadowing, if you will, of richer things to come. I don't know whether or not it was the first time blood was shed. What I know is that *God* covered them. He said, in effect, "Here. Let Me get that for you. Your sad little camo outfit isn't working so well." And even after He did them that great kindness, He knew it wouldn't be enough.

Why the fig leaf among God's treasures? Perhaps to remind

Him—and us—of how very fragile we are, how much we needed Him, how much we need Him still. And of how prone to wander His best and brightest creation was and ever is. As a mother tucks away her baby's smallest outfit, one that it wore for such a brief time and will never wear again, He sees our once-worn leaves, and He smiles. We've long outgrown them. He knew we would. But we're covered just the same.

For while we were still helpless, at the right time Christ died for the ungodly. For one will hardly die for a right-eous man; though perhaps for the good man someone would dare even to die. But God demonstrates His own love toward us, in that while we were yet sinners, Christ died for us. Much more then, having now been justified by His blood, we shall be saved from the wrath of God through Him.

—ROMANS 5:6–9

I sought the LORD, and He answered me,
And delivered me from all my fears.
They looked to Him and were radiant,
And their faces will never be ashamed.

—PSALM 34:4–5

A Fresh Olive Sprig

The God of New Beginnings

Then it came about at the end of forty days, that Noah opened the window of the ark which he had made; and he sent out a raven, and it flew here and there until the water was dried up from the earth. Then he sent out a dove from him, to see if the water was abated from the face of the land; but the dove found no resting place for the sole of her foot, so she returned to him into the ark, for the water was on the surface of all the earth. Then he put out his hand and took her, and brought her into the ark to himself. So he waited yet another seven days; and again he sent out the dove from the ark. The dove came to him toward evening, and behold, in her beak was a freshly picked olive leaf. So Noah knew that the water was abated from the earth.

—GENESIS 8:6–11

The sprig of green from an olive plant is fresh, young, new. It looks to be a seedling, barely sprouted in damp earth before it was plucked up and winged away. Its leaves are longish and thin, with tiny clusters of small white flowers in between. It holds no fruit. It is too young for that. Trees bearing sprigs like this are hardy and prolific, but there was a time when every one of them was destroyed in a rain that seemed to never end.

My two-year-old cavalier King Charles spaniel, Owen, stirred restlessly on the bed, pawing, whining, and otherwise making it impossible for me to remain asleep. A glance at the clock on the bedside table told me it was 3:15 a.m., but even in the dead of night the room was bathed in a weird light. And when I began to orient my sleepy self, I smelled smoke.

At the bedroom window I drew back the curtain and saw two fire trucks parked on the street below, lights flashing but sirens silent. Several crews of firemen were already deploying their equipment. Strange popping noises overhead accelerated my now-anxious movements: pulling on my bathrobe and grabbing my keys, cell phone, and purse. With these few things in hand and Owen on my heels, I opened the door to the hallway, which was filled with the thick smoke I had only smelled before. I clipped my dog's leash onto his collar, closed the front door of my apartment behind me, and ran for the stairs.

From the few neighbors already clustered outside, I learned that one of them, walking his dog a half hour earlier, had seen smoke coming from the building and called 911. In the short time we'd been talking, several more fire trucks had arrived, and soon the street was a congested tangle of vehicles, emergency personnel, and other sleepy residents, rousted not by a whining dog but by shouting firemen banging on their doors. I stopped counting at fourteen trucks, not including those belonging to the media teams that soon swarmed among us. (Note to self and any other interested party: if you do not want to be on the 6:00 a.m. news with bed hair and no makeup, don't sit on the curb, barefoot in a bathrobe with an adorable fire sentry of a spaniel resting in your lap.)

One of the firemen erected a portable command post in the middle of the street, and Owen and I and my next-door neighbors perched behind him, watching as a ladder truck telescoped its ladder, four firemen, and their bulky gear onto the roof right above my living room window. I called my sister and said in hushed disbelief, "I'm okay, but my building's on fire," worrying needlessly that I hadn't locked my door in my haste to leave.

As smoke poured from beneath the roofline, I wondered if I should have collected a few more of my things before I dashed out—my laptop, maybe, or my oldest Bible, or my copy of Elizabeth Barrett Browning's collected poems from G. K. Chesterton's library, with his quirky signature scrawled in its front bookplate. I hadn't been sure there was enough time.

By just after 7:00 a.m. the fire was out, the sun was up, and we were allowed back inside the building. As I topped the stairs and turned down my hallway to see what damage had been done, my jaw dropped. The fire, which had started across the hall and below me in a common room, had climbed the walls to a second-floor electrical closet and spread into the attic above. But the burned-out ceiling, dangling wires, and broken, soggy Sheetrock stopped abruptly less than five feet from my front door. My apartment reeked of smoke, and below the water-stained ceiling my dining table was slightly damp. Smudges and smoky handprints marked the wall where the firemen had entered to see if anyone was still inside, but everything else was just as I had left it hours before.

I was safe, and my things had been spared, although my home would not be habitable for at least sixty days. I hastily packed a few things into a rolling bag and this time locked the door behind me, beginning an odd, unsettling exodus I certainly never planned.

Noah at least got advance warning. He did not wake in the middle of the night to a life-threatening disaster. He saw the flood coming—because the Floodmaker had willingly tipped His hand. God looked upon the world He had made, and saw all evil, all the time. Because of this, the account goes in Genesis, "the LORD was sorry that He had made man on the earth, and He was grieved in His heart" (6:6). The sin that entered the world through Adam and Eve had wounded not just God's good creation but the heart of its Creator as well. His righteousness was offended…but His grace was determined and strong. And when He looked among the mass of fallen humanity for a recipient of that amazing grace, God selected Noah.

Why Noah? We don't know. All the writer of Genesis offers is that "Noah found grace in the eyes of the LORD," and "Noah walked with God" (6:8, 9, NKJV). He wasn't a perfect man. But he *was* wholeheartedly committed to God in a way that must have set him apart from his contemporaries. And God saw it. So He took Noah into His confidence and told him of the plan: "Make yourself an ark of gopherwood; make rooms in the ark, and cover it inside and outside with pitch" (6:14, NKJV).

And Noah did.

At God's direction he constructed a floating houseboat big enough to accommodate his extended family and a teeming menagerie of animals, clean and unclean. The writer of Hebrews says in 11:7 that he did all this "by faith," never having experienced the kind of natural disaster for which he obediently prepared.

And then it rained.

And rained.

And rained.

"The fountains of the great deep burst open, and the floodgates of the sky were opened. The rain fell upon the earth for forty days and forty nights" (7:11–12). On the same day the rains began, Noah, his sons, his wife, and his daughters-in-law entered their lumbering lifeboat, along with every kind of beast and bird and creeping thing there was. Then once they were safely inside, the Lord closed the door of the ark behind them. The floodwaters increased and lifted the ark above the surface of the earth. Mountains were covered. Everything under heaven was covered. And the loss that ensued was devastating: "All flesh that moved on the earth perished, birds and cattle and beasts and every swarming thing…

and all mankind; of all that was on the dry land, all in whose nostrils was the breath of the spirit of life, died" (7:21–22).

All flesh...died.

And the water prevailed on the earth for 150 days.

Then, we're told, "God remembered Noah and all...that were with him in the ark" (8:1). He blew a wind over the earth, and the water began to subside. At the end of another 150 days, the water had decreased—but not yet disappeared. It had been nearly a year since Noah and his entourage first embarked; they could finally see the tops of the mountains again. Thus encouraged, the captain of the craft cracked a window and sent out a raven that flew "here and there" as the water was dried up from the earth. But the raven did not return. Next he dispatched a dove, but finding no place to set its foot down, the dove flew back to him. After seven more days, Noah sent out the dove a second time. This time it "came to him toward evening, and behold, in her beak was a freshly picked olive leaf. So Noah knew that the water was abated from the earth" (8:11).

The ark's passengers had experienced days upon days upon days of nothing but threatening skies and teeming waters. No sign of life beyond the boat where they lived. No breath in the entire world but their own. And then one day, finally, a glimpse of something green. Something alive and growing. It may have been just the smallest sprig of an olive branch—but oh, what it represented! Life. There was more life ahead for Noah and his wife, and his sons

and their wives. It was a brand-new beginning…a gracious one
they had in no way earned.

It takes a while to regain your bearings when you're plucked from
the life you've known. And whether the agent of unwanted change
is a fire or a flood or a frightening diagnosis or an unwanted
breakup or an untimely death—you're as unbalanced as a pitching
boat for more than a little while. I didn't have as much company
as old Noah did, furry or otherwise. Nor as much gear to carry.
But for more than a month, I toted a rolling suitcase and a dog crate
around in my car and depended upon the kindness of friends to
shelter me until I could find a new place to live.

At every stop I had creature comforts that Noah would have
no doubt envied—but like him, I hadn't the slightest idea when
my sojourn would end or precisely where I would find myself
when it did. I longed for familiar things: my favorite coffee mug,
my favorite Bible. The stack of books on my bedside table. Files on
my desktop computer I hadn't copied but wished I had. The steel-
cut oats I like for breakfast and the famous fuzzy bathrobe that now
smelled like old, damp firewood. I missed the comfort of sleeping
in my own bed and showering in my own shower. I missed the ordinary ease of being at home.

Like Noah, though, I had a safe ark in which to travel. I spent
the first two nights with my sister. Three more in an old friend's up-

stairs guest room. A serendipitous housesitting gig found me rambling around for a week in a huge home with Owen and two dogs more than twice his size. (We all adapted well.) A longer string of days was spent in a retreat an hour away from the city…a peaceful change of pace for me and a sweet taste of small-town life. Still another friend and her husband welcomed me in for several days, gave me a key, and encouraged me to come and go as if I were home. They shared their table with me and even embraced Owen in their own petless house, letting him out of his crate for playtime when I was gone. Then a final week of housesitting for more traveling friends was kindly offered, and we were packing up and moving again.

Arks, I discovered, come in all shapes and sizes. But every one of them is weatherproofed by the perfectly dependable pitch of love.

Throughout these stays I searched for another place to live. If I couldn't return to my apartment for two months or more, maybe I could locate something else sooner. Every night, in whatever bed I found myself, I rested my laptop on my knees and pored over screen after screen of online residential listings ("real-estate porn," a wisecracking friend had called my new addiction). One night I entered the zip code of a quaint neighborhood I'd always liked but never imagined I could afford and clicked "New this week." I sat up straighter when a picture of a tiny 1920s Craftsman bungalow with a porch swing popped up.

I clicked through its vitals and hoped it wasn't already leased. My own Realtor friend was out of town for the weekend, but when

I e-mailed the listing to him, he said, "Don't wait for me. Make an appointment with the agent to see it tomorrow if you can. It won't last long." I sent an e-mail to the lister in the middle of the night and called him as soon as the sun was up and the hour was decent. He was also the owner of the house and agreed to show it to me that same day at 11:00. He'd posted it to the Web only minutes before my e-mail, he told me, and I was the first person who'd inquired. I took my sister along to the showing for moral support and knew within five minutes of stepping inside that I'd found home. But there was a catch: it wouldn't be available for another three weeks. I swallowed my momentary disappointment, wrote a check, and signed on the dotted line.

I had more ark-time ahead of me. And an enormous amount of work to do to move my home and office yet again. But I'd seen a tiny, green olive leaf of hope…and it was enough to keep me afloat until I could finally plant new roots in solid ground.

"God remembered Noah," the writer of Genesis reminds us (8:1). Noah was spared from the Flood in a rush of grace stronger than the very waters themselves, and when those waters began to abate, God *remembered* the one He had deliberately saved. I don't believe God's remembering was an unscripted *aha*—the kind of light-bulb epiphany I have when I remember where I last left my keys. It wasn't as if God became so caught up in watery judgment that He completely forgot He had launched an ark and then one day remembered that He had. No, God's remembering was as calculating and well timed as His judgment had been. His remembering was an act of goodness *toward* Noah because of a previous commitment made to him.

God remembered—and kept mercy and grace in His heart for Noah. The green sprig of olive leaf carried to the ark by a dove was proof of what had already been done on Noah's behalf. The waters were receding. Green things were growing. In one single leaf, Noah could see that beyond the wrath of God on the earth, redemption and restoration waited. Despair, if he ever felt it—and he must have during at least a few dark, damp moments—was ameliorated by the promise of God's goodness in the land of the living. He had come a long, wet way, but Noah returned again to a place that felt deeply familiar—only cleaner, fresher, safer, and new.

"We shall not cease from exploration," wrote poet T. S. Eliot, "and the end of all our exploring will be to arrive where we started and know the place for the first time."[1] Noah was finally home.

Thirty-five days after fire sent me packing, grace brought me home too. To an old/new place that feels as if it was waiting just for me. As it was with Noah, my only appropriate response is worship: a shout-out to the One who helped me escape catastrophe, endure exile, and learn all over again my dependence on Him in every circumstance. He made me aware of the flimsy security of walls and windows and doors that lock, and of the utter stability of His arms.

He placed me in an ark of provision and kept me safely there until dry ground was visible again.

He replaced my sorrow with a green and growing hope, and an olive leaf testifies that, with Him, despair is always presumptive.

Praise Him. Praise Him. Praise Him. He remembers His own.

We're no more than a strong thunderstorm or a spark of fire away from disaster. Any of us. This beautiful earth and the life we enjoy on it are much, much more tenuous than they seem. While the rains of God's judgment in Noah's day swept away trees and tents and carved deep scars in the surface of the earth, that same rain yielded, in time, a fresh sprig of olive leaf that smelled like hope. That *was* hope. "The turbulent waters of chaos and nightmare are always threatening to burst forth and flood the earth," writes Frederick Buechner. "We hardly need the tale of Noah to tell us that. The *New York Times* tells us just as well, and our own hearts tell us well too, because chaos and nightmare have their little days there also."[2]

Stuff happens. Life as we know it changes, and not always for the good. But God's love and mercy endure, and where He is, there is always fresh breath and new hope. When Noah held that small leaf in his fingers, he must have felt a holy hush invade his heart. Maybe a tear slid down his cheek—one he didn't brush aside but let fall into his beard and then onto his chest. And then another.

And another. And maybe, just maybe, the fears that had risen in him like a flood abated, too, and a note of praise and thanks rose to his now-practiced lips.

Noah knew, better than he had known before the rain began to fall, the faithfulness of God. And, after the fire, so do I. God needs no bright green branch to prove Himself; He knew all along what He meant to do. But He was good to give that hope to Noah, and good to give it to me. "Into his gracious and puzzling hands we must commend ourselves through all the days of our voyaging," says Buechner. "We must build our arks with love and ride out the storm with courage and know that the little sprig of green in the dove's mouth betokens a reality beyond the storm more precious than the likes of us can imagine."[3]

He is the God of new beginnings, it turns out. And hope really does float, after all.

Because he holds fast to me in love, I will deliver him;
    I will protect him, because he knows my name.
When he calls to me, I will answer him;
    I will be with him in trouble;
    I will rescue him and honor him.
With long life I will satisfy him
    and show him my salvation.

—PSALM 91:14–16, ESV

A Dry Waterskin

The God Who Sees

So Abraham rose early in the morning and took bread and a skin of water and gave them to Hagar, putting them on her shoulder, and gave her the boy, and sent her away. And she departed and wandered about in the wilderness of Beersheba.

When the water in the skin was used up, she left the boy under one of the bushes. Then she went and sat down opposite him, about a bowshot away, for she said, "Do not let me see the boy die." And she sat opposite him, and lifted up her voice and wept.

—Genesis 21:14–16

This dry waterskin served as an ancient thermos—a lifeline against a wanderer's thirst. Made from the hide of an animal, it was soft and flexible when filled...but now its dry and marbled surface feels fragile to the touch. Empty, it is shapeless, useless. But long ago in a desert, it saved the lives of two exiles who thought God had forgotten their whereabouts. He had not.

The house was filling quickly as we settled into our seats at Broadway's Martin Beck Theatre—good seats—rear orchestra, center section. This trip to New York was my graduation gift to my niece, and together we waited expectantly for the opening curtain of the first musical we planned to see: a revival of the 1960s hit *Man of La Mancha,* with Brian Stokes Mitchell in the starring role. Katharine was too young to recognize much of the beautiful music by composer Mitch Leigh—except perhaps the standard "The Impossible Dream"—but she was theater crazy enough to love the sheer beauty of the story and to appreciate its compelling cast of characters.

Soon enough, the houselights went down, and as our eyes adjusted to the scene of a dungeon cell, the first notes of flamenco music began. Magic! Katharine and I sat forward in our seats and stayed there. The charismatic Don Quixote changed everyone he met for the better—but perhaps no one more than his Dulcinea. To the rest of the world she was Aldonza—a weary, hardened woman with no illusions, a woman who sold her body but barricaded her heart. She spat and swore and swung her fists at the men who both bought and bullied her. There was nothing soft about her. Softness was a luxury she could not afford.

But Don Quixote de La Mancha saw something more. From the moment he met her, he addressed Aldonza respectfully as "my lady." He treated her with great honor and insisted that she was really the lady Dulcinea, his sweet one. For her part, she thought him mad. No one was kind to Aldonza. No one cared. But even as she protested his strangely tender treatment, Aldonza couldn't quite shake the thought that someone—even a half-crazy, make-believe knight—saw the woman she had never been…the woman she was afraid to hope to be…and, God help her, the woman she still longed to be. He—and no one else—had called her Dulcinea.

At Don Quixote's deathbed, Aldonza begged the old knight to remember her—to call her by the name he first gave her. He could not speak. But his imminent death seemed to steel her resolve to become the gentle woman only he believed she was. When another at Quixote's bedside called her Aldonza, she straightened herself and said clearly and resolutely, "My name…is Dulcinea."

The woman's name was Hagar. She was an Egyptian…and a slave. Her master was a man named Abram, and he had a barren wife named Sarai. Not contrary to the customs of the day, Hagar was pressed into service to produce an heir for Abram—and as planned, she became pregnant with Abram's child. But although this pregnancy was Sarai's notion, it did not please her to have Hagar in the same household, carrying the child who would be Abram's descendant but not hers.

Author Carolyn Custis James notes that Hagar was "a messy complication in the major plot involving her mistress," "a lost soul right from the start—stuck on the wrong side of the racial divide, uncomfortable inside her own skin, and trapped within a cultural system that stripped her of her rights, her dignity, and her freedom."[1]

Hagar was viewed by Abram and Sarai as little more than a cog in a wheel. She was used by them to achieve their ends and, cut off from her family and her culture, could not help but feel utterly, completely alone. When she became pregnant, she unwisely lorded her pregnancy over her mistress, treating Sarai with a seething contempt. And Sarai, it seems, cared nothing for Hagar's comfort or for the child she carried. Her own failure to produce an heir for Abram had left her more than a little bitter and resentful, emotions she took out on Hagar when the surrogate scheme she'd hatched proved successful. Perhaps feeling guilty for his own actions in this affair, Abram did nothing to ease the tension rife in his household.

Things finally got so bad that Hagar ran away into the wilderness. Sarai did not follow her, and Abram did not seek her out to bring her home. But God knew her whereabouts and met her in her distress:

> The angel of the LORD found her by a spring of water in the wilderness, the spring on the way to Shur. And he said, "Hagar, servant of Sarai, where have you come from and where are you going?" She said, "I am fleeing from my mistress Sarai." The angel of the LORD said to her, "Return to your mistress and submit to her." The angel of the LORD also said to her, "I will surely multiply your offspring so

that they cannot be numbered for multitude." And the angel of the LORD said to her,

"Behold you are pregnant
   and shall bear a son.
You shall call his name Ishmael,
   because the LORD has listened to your affliction."
      (Genesis 16:7–11, ESV)

God saw Hagar. He knew her name. He shared with her the knowledge that she would have a son and that her offspring, too, would be multiplied beyond number. "Hagar," says Carolyn Custis James, "matters deeply to God. She may have been invisible to everyone else, but she was neon bright on God's radar screen.... God focuses on [her] despite the fact that the child she carries is *not* the promised one and her story is only a messy interruption to the *real* story God is weaving."[2]

In response to God's wilderness overture to Hagar, she gave him a name: "You are a God of seeing," she said. "Truly here I have seen him who looks after me" (16:13, ESV).

Like Hagar, I was once a participant in a kingdom enterprise. For ten years, I served on the staff of the church I had attended (and taught at) from early adulthood. Not quite midway through my

tenure there, I was moved to a spot where I mostly made myself useful doing research for sermons and writing television spots, Sunday bulletin letters, ads, magazine articles, and so forth. I loved to write, but I never aspired to be anyone's ghostwriter. Then one day the phone rang and I was asked, "Do you think you could ghostwrite a book for me?" I quickly said yes (I thought of it as a dozen or so long term papers) and then wondered what in the world I might have gotten myself into.

Ghosting became a hands-on tutorial that proved incredibly valuable for me, and I suppose it was valuable for the ministry too. At least I hope it was. I didn't even mind being an invisible author—but after six years and five books, it had become a very lonely way to work. I was single. I lived alone. And most days I worked in my office for eight hours or more, with little or no interaction with anyone but the janitor who came each day to empty my trash. I missed the give-and-take of teamwork and longed for more involvement and less isolation.

Imagining that I had the freedom to ask for what I needed, I did, explaining that I wanted to continue writing as I had been but perhaps add more team projects for some much-needed collaboration. Shortly thereafter I found myself in another staff member's office while my boss was away on vacation, being briefed on my new job—all the while receiving phone calls from the person who would evidently soon be handling the duties I loved most, asking me for guidance on how to prepare manuscripts, book proposals, and so forth. It was a confusing time, but the message was clear if not exactly direct—I was being moved out. Whether my previous request was viewed as inappropriate or not, I never knew. But what happened as a result felt an awful lot like being disowned.

The wilderness I was banished to wasn't far away—a two-story metal building across the parking lot—but it was another world altogether. My things were loaded up and dispatched, and for three months the reference books from the shelves of my previous office sat in a large plastic garbage bin in the middle of the floor. There was no place to store them in my new department, and no one seemed able to tell me whether or not I was allowed to order shelves.

Like Hagar, I longed to run for the hills and not look back. And as He had said to Hagar, God said, "No, go back and submit." So I stayed put. For six months I labored with a wonderfully talented team to produce a monthly magazine, print ads, and other communication materials, and we did good work. But I couldn't shake the feeling of being cut loose after I'd poured out my heart and soul for nearly a decade.

It hurt to go to work. It hurt to sit in the pew on Sunday. I felt abandoned and even a little ashamed, but after six months of licking my wounds, I felt God release me to go. I returned to corporate life, where the pay was nearly twice as high and my expectations were blessedly low. I wondered more than once if this was how divorce felt. I continued to teach every other Sunday, but after my class, instead of going with friends into worship, I would get in my car alone, turn on the live radio broadcast of the morning service, and drive the 610 Loop around the city until the closing hymn was sung. It was as close as I could get to worship in the community I loved without my heart breaking.

Hagar fled to the wilderness, not once, but twice. Thirteen years after Ishmael was born, her master and mistress—now renamed Abraham and Sarah—rejoiced at the birth of Isaac, the son and heir long promised by God. If Hagar thought the arrival of this son would temper her mistress's resentment, she was mistaken. Genesis tells us, "The child grew and was weaned. And Abraham made a great feast on the day that Isaac was weaned. But Sarah saw the son of Hagar the Egyptian, whom she had borne to Abraham, laughing. So she said to Abraham, 'Cast out this slave woman with her son, for the son of this slave woman shall not be heir with my son Isaac'" (21:8–10, ESV). Abraham didn't want anything to do with the conflict, but God spoke to him saying, "Whatever Sarah says to you, do as she tells you, for through Isaac shall your offspring be named" (21:12, ESV).

Sarah had asked Abraham to banish Hagar and her son, Ishmael, so her husband complied. He arose early in the morning, took some bread and a skin of water, and sent Hagar and Ishmael away with them. The two of them wandered in the wilderness of Beersheba until all the water was gone and Hagar feared they would both die. She made Ishmael as comfortable as she could under a large bush and sat down a good distance away from him, reasoning that she did not want to be near enough to watch her son slowly die of thirst.

She must have felt invisible. But God saw her again.

As she began to weep, God heard Hagar and heard the voice of the boy. At Hagar's absolute lowest moment, an angel of God called to her from heaven, saying, "What troubles you, Hagar? Fear not, for God has heard the voice of the boy where he is. Up! Lift up the boy, and hold him fast with your hand, for I will make him into a great nation" (21:17–18, ESV).

The angel of God didn't stop with a distant "attagirl" from on high either—as encouraging as words must have been. No. All-seeing God also opened the eyes of desperate Hagar, and she saw a well of water that must have been there all along. Maybe she had even glanced at it before and simply moved on, assuming it was as dry and empty as she was. Redirected to the well, she filled the parched waterskin with fresh, soothing water and gave her son a drink. And she drank in the knowledge that the God she'd once named El Roi, or "the one who sees," had seen her in her first flight and was seeing her still.

Aldonza felt invisible until Don Quixote looked on her and called her Dulcinea. Each time Hagar found herself alone and abandoned in the wilderness, God called her by name. When I left the ministry I thought I might serve in for life, I felt invisible too. I wasn't sure I had the strength or courage to become an integral part of another church. I felt caught between one door that had closed and another I was waiting for God to open. But He knew my whereabouts, and He did not allow me to dwell in isolation for long. When He did call me to another place, it was to a fledgling congregation smaller than my previous Sunday-school class. But almost instantly, I knew I belonged.

"God doesn't call us to himself," writes Carolyn Custis James, "without also calling us to his people. It is a mixed blessing for all of us, for the church isn't always the safest place. The people there aren't necessarily the ones we would choose for our friends, and, sadly, some of our most painful wounds come from our relationships with other believers. But these are the people we need and who also need us. We come to know God better and grow stronger as Christians when we are joined to the community of his people and we work together to know him."[3]

I could have slipped away to my new church home without anyone really knowing I was gone. But there was something else I needed, something I longed for but didn't think I might have. I needed a blessing. A benediction. I wanted someone who knew my story in that place to release me and tell me it was good for me to go. I made an appointment to speak to a senior pastor on the staff—a wise and compassionate elder statesman and friend who had taught, exhorted, encouraged, and even lovingly corrected me for years. I planned to tell him of my decision in the hope that it would at least be understood and accepted with goodwill.

I got so much more than I'd allowed myself to hope for. After a casual dinner, this pastor, his wife, and I settled in to his study for a visit. I shared with them my plans and what I felt God calling me to do. Then I waited for his response. What that pastor said assured me again that God did, in fact, see me…and that as lost as I had felt, I had never been lost to Him.

"Leigh," he said, "you are like a daughter to us. And you and I will always be a part of the fellowship of the saints together, no matter what church you're in or what church I'm in. We're family. And you must—you must!—go where you believe God is calling you." I felt as though I had finally stumbled onto a well and been given a long drink of cold water in a dry, hot place. But my friend didn't stop there. "I want to pray for you," he said, and without hesitating, he did. The three of us in that small upper-room study came together for a few precious moments as the body of Christ— the church—and I received the blessing I had hungered for, even without my asking for it.

"The gospel," says pastor and writer Eugene Peterson, "does not address a faceless, nameless mob, but persons. The history of salvation is thick with names."[4] Names like Abraham, Sarah, and

Isaac. Rebekah, Jacob, and Esau. Names like Hagar and Ishmael. And like mine.

A friend asked me once, "If God had a name for you that would embody the new person He is making of you through His love, what would that name be?" I thought then of Don Quixote, and how he gave the coarse, bitter Aldonza the name Dulcinea— "sweet one." And I told him I thought God might lovingly call me "My unforgettable tattoo" because He says my identity is ever before Him, carved on the palms of His hands (see Isaiah 49:16).

In the flyleaf of another writer's book, C. S. Lewis wrote:

It is not an abstraction called Humanity that is to be saved. It is you…your soul, and, in some sense yet to be understood, even your body, that was made for the high and holy place. All that you are…every fold and crease of your individuality was devised from all eternity to fit God as a glove fits a hand. All that intimate particularity which you can hardly grasp yourself, much less communicate to your fellow creatures, is no mystery to Him. He made those ins and outs that He might fill them.[5]

In the years since I left my longtime spiritual home, I have been back many times. I have taught, worshiped, mourned, laughed, and celebrated in the place where my faith grew up. Each time, I have thanked God for my years there—for the relationships made, the lessons learned, and the service it was my privilege to offer. It was both good for me to be there and good for me to go. God has His plans for those still serving there, and for me. I am grateful for His loving care of me, both then and now.

Like Hagar, I have a God who knows my name. A God who sees. I have never been lost to Him—and neither have you. The scrap of an old waterskin remains to tell the story. He sees. He knows your story. You are His. He has His plans for you. He has long been in the business of naming names, and oh how He loves the sound of yours!

Can a mother forget the baby at her breast
    and have no compassion on the child she has borne?
Though she may forget,
    I will not forget you!
See, I have engraved you on the palms of my hands;
    your walls are ever before me.

—ISAIAH 49:15–16, NIV

Abraham's Knife

The God Who Provides

When they came to the place of which God had told him, Abraham built the altar there and laid the wood in order and bound Isaac his son and laid him on the altar, on top of the wood. Then Abraham reached out his hand and took the knife to slaughter his son. But the angel of the LORD called to him from heaven and said, "Abraham, Abraham!" And he said, "Here am I." He said, "Do not lay your hand on the boy or do anything to him, for now I know that you fear God, seeing you have not withheld your son, your only son, from me.

—GENESIS 22:9–12, ESV

The blade is shaped of flint, its knapped edge honed to cutting strength. An ancient tribesman would have used it to hunt and kill his prey, protecting himself and providing food. Its weight is substantial. . .and to a man commanded to take it and kill his son, it must have seemed heavier still. The rough tool is stained, too, with the accumulated proof of every deep wound it has made. It was clean only once, and that was many, many years ago.

I only ever aspired to one thing, really: to be a good man's wife. All my earliest role models were wives—the grandmothers, mother, aunts, family friends, and teachers who unwittingly shaped my view of womanhood. I did not know, growing up, even one never-married adult woman who lived on her own and followed Jesus. Not one. No one who knew me then would have predicted I would be that woman, and frankly I wouldn't have either. Now I shake my head in wonder when I meet ex-boyfriends' wives and children at the mall or at a restaurant, or when I open the mailbox to find graduation and wedding invitations from the adult offspring of my childhood playmates.

More than once I've looked back at the string of mostly wonderful men I have loved and wondered how it is that not one of them chose me to be his wife. In my more introspective moments, I try to identify the secret ingredient that has kept me single thus far and to determine if it will always be so. Too opinionated perhaps? Too competitive or independent? Not pretty or playful or accommodating enough, or (as has been suggested more than once) a little too picky for my own good?

The truth is, I didn't just imagine marriage and children; I expected them—and believed I would have them. They were—and in some ways still are—the strongest desires of my heart. And I have delighted myself for a very long time in my Lord.

If it weren't too painfully cynical, I could craft a pretty funny stand-up routine using the lines I've heard offered to explain more disappointing breakups than I'd like to admit. Lines like, "I want to marry someone just like you who's Lebanese," or, "I wish I was as sure about one thing as you are about everything." (Ouch.) Or, "I really do love you, just not the way you should love someone you want to marry." (How exactly is that? I'm still not sure.) The unoriginal but no less annoying "I'm not good enough for you" has been invoked more than once—and I'm inclined to advise anyone on the receiving end of this one simply to believe its claimant and move on. But perhaps my all-time favorite parting explanation is, "I'm like the dog that chased the car and caught it. I'm not sure what to do with you." I wish now I had been quick enough to reply with a line stolen from Shakespeare's *Henry V:* "Can any of your neighbours tell?"[1]

I used to think that marriage was every good Christian girl's entitlement. Now I see that it is really a gift of grace and that a good and lasting union is a rare gift indeed. I once believed that God's promised blessings would flow to me through this means and hardly entertained any other possibility. It has taken my heart a long time to trust more in divine provision than in human entitlement.

Abraham wasn't left to wonder how God meant to bless him. God had made it clear: "Behold, My covenant is with you, and you will be the father of a multitude of nations.... I will establish My covenant between Me and you and your descendants after you throughout their generations for an everlasting covenant, to be God to you and to your descendants after you.... Sarah your wife will bear you a son, and you shall call his name Isaac" (Genesis 17:4, 7, 19).

Abraham and Sarah were plenty old. They'd heard this wild promise before—or at least pieces of it through the years. But they weren't getting any younger, and God wasn't changing His story. The gap between the promise and any reasonable human means of its fulfillment had grown impossibly wide. Was it time to put their hopes away? To conclude they'd confused the plan somehow or strayed too far from it for God to keep His word? And now He was naming this promise, calling him Isaac—"laughter." Who was the joke on? Who would have the last laugh?

But a year later Isaac was indeed born. Abraham was one hundred years old, with Sarah not far behind. *Laughter* seemed the perfect name for this shock-the-neighbors baby boy. "Sarah said, 'God has made laughter for me; everyone who hears will laugh with me.' And she said, 'Who would have said to Abraham that Sarah would nurse children? Yet I have borne him a son in his old age'" (21:6–7).

Finally, after years of trusting, waiting, and believing, they were a happy family of three. God had made good on His promise, and there would be no more uncertainty, no more confusion, and no more childless heartache for Abraham and Sarah. They could finally pull their rockers together on the porch and watch Isaac grow up, marry, and give them grandchildren if he hurried. Right? Well, no. Not exactly.

Abraham would learn the hard way that God reserves the right to test the faith of His people by calling them to obey Him in ways that seem inexplicable. Beyond reason. And in Abraham's case, as wild and unthinkable as the original promises he was given.

One day—a day that dawned like any other ordinary day—God said these stunning words to His servant Abraham: "Take your son, your only son Isaac, whom you love, and go to the land of Moriah, and offer him there as a burnt offering on one of the mountains of which I shall tell you" (22:2, ESV). With this single command, God closed all the loopholes. "Take your son," He said. "Not Hagar's or another servant's. Yours. And not your son Ishmael—the one you tried to substitute once before. Take the boy I promised and gave: Isaac. Don't bother reminding Me he is the only son of promise. I am aware that you have no other. And don't wonder if I could be somehow unaware of your deep, deep love for him. I know well how much you love him. Offer Isaac. Not as a living, breathing sacrifice but as a complete, no-way-out sacrifice: slain, bled to death, and burned to ashes. Don't say you don't know where, Abraham, or when. I will show you. Your only job is obedience. Take your son, follow Me, and climb."

So Abraham did.

The greatest test in Abraham's life came after he had finally received the promise. He was no stranger to God, and God was no stranger to him. They'd been through a lot together. Abraham had seen plenty. He'd experienced the thrill of obedience, the hope of promise, the satisfaction of faith rewarded. He'd made a few slips, to be sure. But the overriding theme of his life was one of following hard after the God who first beckoned him out of Ur and into mystery.

From what Abraham could tell, God had set his future—and the future of a host of promised descendants—on Isaac. And now God was asking him to sacrifice this same boy. He could not possibly reconcile the Almighty's former promise with His present command. So the question became this: would he cling to what God had given, or would he cling to God alone? If all of Abraham's hopes were in Isaac, then all his hopes could be lost. But if all his hopes were in the God who promised and provided Isaac, he could go on hoping in the face of anything—even this.

A friend and I were sharing dinner to celebrate the arrival of the bright orange and blue FedEx envelope that contained my first published book. We excitedly passed the one copy between us as we waited for our food, and I was feeling a little giddy over its arrival. I even liked the way its fresh, new pages smelled as I cracked the spine and pressed my face into them.

When I looked away from the book, I saw a family of four coming through the door of the casual neighborhood eatery we had chosen: a dad, a mom, and two little boys. Only this wasn't just any dad. This was a man I'd spent nearly seven years of my life off and on longing for—one who'd more than once nursed my bruised heart back to health after others had broken it, and who had made a pact with me that if either of us eventually married someone else, we wouldn't let the other hear it through the grapevine. We'd telephone with our good news and be glad in it together. Only, when his turn came, he didn't call. I learned of his plans to wed from his sister-in-law, who spoke of it as if I already knew.

Now nearly six years had passed, years in which we hadn't once been face to face. (I had avoided his home-from-the-honeymoon phone calls; I didn't think it was wise to rehash the past with someone else's brand-new husband. Instead, I sent a polite card of congratulations to them both, along with a nice wedding gift.)

Now there was no way out of the restaurant without passing within a few feet of his happy family dinner. I tried to ignore them while we finished our food, but I kept involuntarily glancing in their direction—studying the woman who'd captured my friend's heart without my even knowing and looking at two beautiful brown-eyed boys who might have been mine. My friend and I prolonged the inevitable gauntlet by ordering after-dinner coffees, but finally we couldn't linger any longer. After I stuffed my book in my bag, we paid our tab and headed for the door. He saw us coming—I'm fairly certain he'd spotted us as soon as he'd arrived.

As we neared their table, I prepared to take my cue from him: if he looked down or away, I would pass by without a greeting. The call was his to make. He raised his head, made eye contact, and smiled a little. I stopped and said as brightly as I could, "Well, hey there. How are you?"

"Good, good," he replied. Then, "Leigh, have you ever met my wife?"

I rejected the unflattering response that first jumped to my lips, smiled back, and said, "Why no, I don't believe I have." Nothing in his tone indicated to her whether I might have been a business acquaintance, a long-lost college friend, or something more awkward. He quickly introduced his spouse, then each adorable boy in turn. (They had biblical names.) Forcing my pinched face to soften, I smiled at her and said without hesitating, "It's a pleasure to meet you. And you have a beautiful family." Then I ducked my head and was out the door clean before the tears came. But not by much.

Years ago, when it became apparent that the life I'd prayed for with this man was not to be, I ripped pages of prayers and pleadings about him from my journals, reduced them to tiny little pieces of paper, and burned them all. Not in anger but willfully, prayerfully, as an offering to God. I kept the ashes in a small glass box on my dresser to remind me each day that this was a hope I had relinquished back to Him. But as Elisabeth Elliot likes to say, "Living sacrifices have a way of crawling right off the altar." My dreams might have been reduced to ashes, but my heart still quickened at the chance sight of him, or the sound of his soothing voice.

Emily Dickinson read my fickle emotions like a third-grade book when she penned these heart-wise words:

Long Years apart—can make no
Breach a second cannot fill—
The absence of the Witch does not
Invalidate the spell—

The embers of a Thousand Years
Uncovered by the Hand
That fondled them when they were Fire
Will stir and understand.[2]

I had resolved to move on. And move on I did. But my heart failed to release its grip on the old dream. I didn't have a family. My friend did. And until that ill-fated evening at the restaurant, I hadn't realized how stubbornly I still clung to that desire. It is a far, far easier thing to believe God's good intentions toward you when you're holding Isaac's hand in yours. His reputation as the God who provides is not so hard to trust when that provision is standing before you in plain sight. What kind of God asks those He loves to sacrifice the things dearest to them, even gifts that He Himself has promised or bestowed?

Well, mine does, actually.

C. S. Lewis says, "In love, He claims all. There's no bargaining with Him."[3] And He is well within His rights to do so.

After Abraham heard God's chilling command, he obeyed. He saddled his donkey, took two of his young men with him, and called for his son Isaac. He cut the wood for the burnt offering himself and began moving in the direction God pointed him. On the third day he saw his destination from afar and said to the young men, "Stay here with the donkey; I and the boy will go over there and worship and come again to you" (Genesis 22:5, ESV). Then he laid the wood on Isaac's back and carried in his own hands the fire and the knife. Isaac must have heard Abraham's words—but he had a question: "My father! Behold, the fire and the wood, but where is the lamb for the burnt offering?" What these innocent words did to Abraham's heart we are not told. His reply to his son was simply, "God will provide for Himself the lamb for the burnt offering" (22:7–8).

What a smooth operator old Abraham was! By deferring Isaac's question to God, he invited the Almighty into his terrible test and protected his son as long as he could from the knowledge of his own intent. Abraham knew what he would do—but he did not yet know what God might do. Søren Kierkegaard writes, "There he stood, the old man, with his only hope! But he did not doubt, he did not look anxiously to the right or to the left, he did not challenge heaven with his prayers. He knew that it was God the Almighty who was trying him…but he knew also that no sacrifice was too hard when God required it—and he drew the knife."[4]

When Abraham drew his knife, he meant to bring it down. God knew his intent—and that was enough. Abraham's trusting belief was the thing that allowed him to obey without question and to sacrifice without reservation. He had no power over the test or its outcome. When God was his only hope, God became his best hope.

It is ever so with us.

Have I laid my Isaac down on the pyre? Raised the knife on the life I believed I was made for? I have. More than once. The tests still come, though not as fiercely and frequently as they once did. I do believe that God can accomplish all He has planned for me with or without marriage, and with or without a family of my own. Does my heart still yearn for those things? It does. But maybe it's the longing that makes every ensuing trip up Mount Moriah full of meaning—each time distilling my long history with Him down to a single, telling moment with a knife held high.

In the end, the blade of that knife is always stained. But in Abraham's story and in mine, the blood of sacrifice is provided—not by Abraham, or by me, but by God Himself. He has been, and will always be for me, the God who gives in love what love requires. All He asks is that I love the Giver more than any gift He may bestow. So far at least, I believe that I do.

> What then shall we say to these things? If God is for us, who can be against us? He who did not spare his own Son but gave him up for us all, how will he not also with him graciously give us all things?
>
> —ROMANS 8:31–32, ESV

> By faith Abraham, when he was tested, offered up Isaac, and he who had received the promises was in the act of offering up his only son, of whom it was said, "Through Isaac shall your offspring be named." He considered that God was able even to raise him from the dead, from which, figuratively speaking, he did receive him back.
>
> —HEBREWS 11:17–19, ESV

5

A Strip of Bloodied Cloth

The God with a Bigger Plan

They took Joseph's tunic, and slaughtered a male goat and dipped the tunic in the blood; and they sent the varicolored tunic and brought it to their father and said, "We found this; please examine it to see whether it is your son's tunic or not." Then he examined it and said, "It is my son's tunic. A wild beast has devoured him; Joseph has surely been torn to pieces!" So Jacob tore his clothes, and put sackcloth on his loins and mourned for his son many days.

—GENESIS 37:31–34

The cloth is rolled up like a bandage. It might have been quite colorful when it was new. Today its hues have faded to an indistinct blur, no color clearly identifiable save one: a brick-brown stain that proves, when the strip of fabric is unrolled, to be quite large. Whatever—or whoever—lost blood enough to make this stain almost surely died as a result. What sort of tragedy did this wrap once cover—and is there any way the story could have ended well?

I'm a nester. I've yet to own a piece of real estate or sign my name to a thirty-year mortgage note, but every spot I've landed in I have set out to make uniquely mine.

The space I most adored in a long line of so-so rentals was the lower half of a 1936 duplex in a neighborhood where every tree-lined street bore a British writer's name. When I saw the For Lease sign tucked inside the front window of the neat red brick on Addison, I was charmed and convinced. I knew with one look that it would become my home.

The flat's ample size—sixteen hundred square feet for one girl and her smallish dog—felt luxurious. Its weathered hardwood floors cracked and popped from years of steady footsteps, and every window looked out on something green. A laughable lack of closet space was offset by a kitchen large enough to roller-skate through and more cabinets than I ever managed to fill, even after seven years of housekeeping.

I had real neighbors on Addison Street—and we knew each other by name. We chatted outside in the evenings and watched over one another's homes when someone was away. I bought scads of Girl Scout cookies and wrapping paper from the half-dozen school-age girls on our block, and I stopped on cue on the sidewalk as they ran toward me, squealing, "Owen!" on regular spaniel-walking outings. (They also knew me as "Miss Leigh," but more than anything else, I was the woman who held adorable Owen's leash.)

It was on Addison that I healed from one bruised and broken heart and the kinder scars of two surgeries, wrote my first two books and began a third, nursed a hopelessly sick pet and grieved his death, welcomed and trained a new puppy, survived two mid-career job changes, and finally launched a business of my own. During that same span I endured twenty-four months of near-constant overhead construction ("Six months max," my new landlord had promised), an unexpected roof replacement, *and* a jarring foundation repair—all without complaint. Two years after I moved in, I gained an upstairs neighbor, and a good one. I didn't even mind that I would now be parking on the street to leave the driveway open for her sleek navy Jaguar. (It was low enough to the ground to fit into the tiny, pre–World War II garage; my older, American-made SUV was not.)

I'd planned to leave someday, of course. The previous tenant had been an aging spinster who died in her eighties watching television in the sunroom—not a model I hoped to emulate. I toyed with the idea of buying something and had even begun to look, although not earnestly. I was comfortable in my neighborhood. I felt safe on its streets. But when the time came to renew my lease again, my landlord was uncharacteristically silent. My upstairs co-dweller had already received a stuffed, leaselike envelope from him, and I had not. (Our mail was dropped into a common stairwell, to be sorted out by whoever arrived home first.) One day she casually asked if I had noticed the nice place for lease at the end of the block.

I told her I hadn't. She seemed to think perhaps I should take a look.

A few days later I mentioned her not-so-random comment during a phone conversation with our landlord and inquired about his plans. Confronted, he owned up. He was not renewing my lease because he planned to return from out of state, newly divorced, and live in the downstairs half of the duplex himself.

Even though I'd lived there longer than my upstairs neighbor.

Even though our leases expired at the same time.

Even though I'd endured his protracted construction madness and made repairs on my own dime when he insisted I do so.

He then matter-of-factly announced the date of his return, leaving me less than sixty days to reimagine my residence and my life. That would have been troubling enough, but after I scrambled to find a new (and in no way nearly as delightful) place to land, co-ordinated a move I didn't want, *and* took pains to leave everything spotless and in good working order, he refused to refund a single dime of the hefty deposit he'd held for seven years, citing undue wear and tear on the unsealed hardwood floors I'd already repaired once. He did this not in person or by phone but in an e-mail with attached photographs of the spots he deemed excessively worn, along with an outrageous estimate from a flooring company to refinish the en-tire duplex—for more than twice the amount he owed me.

Then, according to my upstairs neighbor when she offered to advise me in small-claims court protocol (she was a litigator by trade), "He rented a sander for forty dollars a day and did the work himself. He didn't even hire someone to help him, and it took him less than a week."

My deeply ingrained sense of justice took a hard blow; my stomach churned every time I thought of what I'd lost. Months passed before I could drive anywhere near my old address without experiencing waves of negative emotion. I felt taken advantage of, and I believed I did not deserve the treatment I got. Worst of all, alone, in quiet moments, I wondered why my good God had let things happen in this way when He surely knew how much I loved my little home.

The old man clutches a bloodied scrap of cloth in his callused hands. Ten sons stand mute before him, aloof to the tears that wet their father's cheeks and lips and beard. They know and hide the ugly truth: a hated brother left to die in the wilderness, then sold to slave traders. They allow their brokenhearted father to believe that his favorite boy is dead, attacked by a wild animal instead of sabotaged by his own siblings.

In an ancient family drama dysfunctional enough to merit a video-recorded stint in the Dr. Phil House, Jacob and his sons stand at odds, long years away from truth telling. A family once filled with promise is fractured instead by lies and deceit.

And where is God?

Where is the heralded Father of Abraham and of Isaac? The God who spoke to Jacob at Bethel and touched his thigh at the Jabbok River, who promised him the moon and stars, and Canaan too, for that matter? How can this good and watchful God allow His own handpicked patriarch to endure such terrible loss? Jacob's livestock he can do without, and he has wives to spare. But Joseph? Joseph is the firstborn child of his one true love—his beautiful Rachel—the woman whose eyes had made him sure of how it felt to lose his heart and gain the world. Dear Joseph, son of precious Rachel. Now dead. Gone.

Hard evidence doesn't lie, does it?

The tunic held out for Jacob's examination belongs to Joseph. His father remembers its colors well, for he had selected each one himself. Bright green. Gold. Purple. Crimson. Brilliant blue. And day by day he had watched the fabric take shape on a wooden frame. Warp and woof crossed over and under again at right angles, building shape and pattern into the cloth that would cover his young boy's shoulders like the mantle of the king. Oh, there can be no mistaking it. This is young Joseph's coat. And the stain on it is blood—no doubt of that either. Jacob is shepherd enough to know blood when he sees it. How many lambs has he birthed and slain himself? How many of his own cloaks have borne this same rusty stain? Now here is his boy's coat…and on it, too much blood to hope that he might have escaped whatever terror befell him. Jacob wishes with a father's breaking heart that the blood could have been his own, not Joseph's, and pressing the ruined cloth to his mouth, he sobs great, heaving cries of grief and loss.

So ends a true and tragic story. The screen fades to black. Haunting music soars and credits roll. Only, Joseph's disappearance was *not* the end—just a pause before more jagged twists and turns. The conspiring brothers presented hard evidence to substantiate their lies. And for a time at least, their tall tale was undisputed. But the Jacob-and-Joseph story wasn't nearly over. Jacob's God had in mind a bigger plan. And so does mine.

Make no mistake: I am as undone as Jacob when I am deceived or unfairly treated. I have no Teflon coating to repel life's hurts. Some people may relish suffering, enjoying the inevitable sympathy tossed their way as a result. Let the record show that I am not such a person. When I am wronged or falsely accused or intentionally wounded, my first impulse is not to settle in with sorrow but to protest. Not to surrender, but to defend myself, or even retaliate. I do not bear ill treatment long or well. I know I am supposed to turn the other cheek—but my neck seems to stiffen when I try.

Thankfully, the I AM is a patient and steady weaver of stories. Undeterred by injustice or abuse or deceit (or perhaps with the aid of it), He sees with the trifocal sharpness of omniscience what has been, what is, and what is yet to be. Time and circumstance are neat skeins of thread at the foot of His throne, and He wisely intersects one strand with another to form a perfect whole. Contrasting hues only add drama and depth to His work: A bright string of joy is crossed by a dark thread of pain. Triumph meets disaster. Love passes over indifference. Power intersects weakness. Gratification covers yearning. Doubt interlaces with belief. Hope extends out beyond despair. Each thread is distinct. Each one is real. The evidence doesn't lie…but the story isn't done.

I did not want to budge from my nest on Addison Street. I loved my little home. It had become a place of refuge where I was committed to loving and serving God. It fit me like a glove. But I'm not writing the story—and I can't foresee what twists and turns it will take before the Storyteller is done. I wanted the ease and comfort of a well-worn, familiar home. He clearly meant for me to move beyond that—and He is the God with a bigger plan. My heart (and my bank account) took a pretty significant hit. I wondered if God did indeed have my back. I still wish I could have stayed there longer, even though I know the story isn't done yet. Not by a long shot.

Years after his heartbreaking loss, Jacob would stand before his boy Joseph, in Egypt of all places. He would see his fractured family reunited, and his grief would finally fade in the joy of Joseph's strong embrace. No doubt he would also see in retrospect the painstaking work of God that made it so. In the course of this plot that thickened, God's chosen ones would take up residence in a foreign land where they would prosper and multiply until the time was ripe for yet another chapter in the history of grace. Because this God of ours has a bigger plan.

It's bigger than our own sins and the sins perpetrated against us. I know this. I've seen it proved in myriad ways, and still...the evidence frequently hints otherwise. Those scraps of bloodied cloth that dot the landscape of my own story can, and sometimes do, cause my faith to waver. I tremble before lies. Lost opportunities. Sickness. Death. Separation. Rejection. Failure. Examining even one of these bloody cloths forces up from my fearful heart questions I can't answer. When they appear in combination (and they frequently do), I am hurt and confused. I know in my head that the story is not over, that the plan of God is not yet complete...but my heart struggles to press on in faith, to believe that He is crafting a truer, richer tale.

Not so with Joseph. He never seemed to stop believing that God knew his whereabouts. That his brothers' ill treatment was not the truest (or even the most interesting) thing about him. Years later—years of hardship but also of blessing and success in a foreign place—Joseph believed enough in the plan of God to let his brothers off the hook. And they never saw that goodness coming:

Joseph said to his brothers, "Please come closer to me." And they came closer. And he said, "I am your brother Joseph, whom you sold into Egypt. Now do not be grieved or

angry with yourselves, because you sold me here, for God
sent me before you to preserve life.… God sent me before
you to preserve for you a remnant in the earth, and to keep
you alive by a great deliverance. Now, therefore, it was not
you who sent me here, but God; and He has made me a
father to Pharaoh and lord of all his household and ruler
over all the land of Egypt." (Genesis 45:4–5, 7–8)

I know there is more to Jacob's story—and Joseph's—because
I have the privilege of hindsight. I know the story that began in Ur
with a man named Abraham ultimately reached its climax in Judea
with the sacrificial death and resurrection of God's own Son. In
Abraham's seed, Jesus, God defeated sin and death for all eternity,
making Satan's claims on me at best only temporary, his grip on this
world fleeting. And I know that in the resolution of the grand story,
Christ will rule, and we with Him. All that God has ordained will
be accomplished, and He will not be forced to revise His story one
iota by lesser powers than He. Because Jesus, too, wore a bloodied
coat—and for three long days it appeared as if the end of everything
good had come. But sometimes the evidence lies.

How do I know this? I confess, I've read ahead:

He will dwell among them, and they shall be His people,
and God Himself will be among them, and He will wipe
away every tear from their eyes; and there will no longer be

any death; there will no longer be any mourning, or crying, or pain. (Revelation 21:3–4)

Because of Jesus, my temporary hurts and disappointments can never do what Satan has hoped they would: they can never shut me off from the pursuing love of God. That's why I'm more hopeful than hesitant as I read these words from Paul:

Who will separate us from the love of Christ? Will tribulation, or distress, or persecution, or famine, or nakedness, or peril, or sword? Just as it is written,

"For Your sake we are being put to death all day long; We were considered as sheep to be slaughtered."

But in all these things we overwhelmingly conquer through Him who loved us. (Romans 8:35–37)

Not in *spite* of all these things—*in* all these things! All evidence to the contrary, God is at work in the very parts of the story we'd most like to skip over. He is at work in tribulation, distress, persecution, and famine. In the vulnerability of nakedness, in the threat of peril, and in the bloodshed from the sword. "I shall know why," writes poet Emily Dickinson, "when time is over, / And I have ceased to wonder why; / Christ will explain *each separate anguish* / In the fair schoolroom of the sky."[1]

No explanation is given here for unfair treatment or egregious injustice. God offers no ready alibi for His whereabouts when our world is being rattled like a bag of bones. But He doesn't need to. Because He is—and has always been—the God with a bigger plan.

Perhaps one day, in eternity, I'll finger scraps of bloodied cloth with Him and no longer see them as reminders of injustices, tragedies, or wrongs done against me but as redeemed treasures of memory for Him and me alone to share. He'll remind me from His own Son's story that the truest answers are always written in blood. And that the story—the best one, the real one—is still unfolding, line by heart-hammering, faith-stretching line.

I know the plans I have for you, declares the LORD,
plans for welfare and not for evil, to give you a future
and a hope. Then you will call upon me and come and
pray to me, and I will hear you. You will seek me and
find me, when you seek me with all your heart.

—JEREMIAH 29:11–13, ESV

What then shall we say to these things? If God is for us,
who can be against us? He who did not spare his own
Son but gave him up for us all, how will he not also
with him graciously give us all things?

—ROMANS 8:31–32, ESV

6

A Bloodstained Piece of Wood

The God Who Defeats Death

Tell all the congregation of Israel that on the tenth day of this month every man shall take a lamb according to their fathers' houses, a lamb for a household.... And you shall keep it until the fourteenth day of this month, when the whole assembly of the congregation of Israel shall kill their lambs at twilight.

Then they shall take some of the blood and put it on the two doorposts and the lintel of the houses in which they eat it.... For I will pass through the land of Egypt that night, and I will strike all the firstborn in the land of Egypt, both man and beast; and on all the gods of Egypt I will execute judgments: I am the LORD. The blood shall be a sign for you, on the houses where you are. And when I see the blood, I will pass over you.

—EXODUS 12:3, 6–7, 12–13, ESV

Just a small piece of wood that once framed the doorway of a home. Removed from that context, it seems ordinary, even inconsequential. The only thing unusual about it is its markings—the spraylike spots and streaks that suggest something was once splashed upon it haphazardly. But the painter of this relic could not have been more deliberate, more particular. His "paint" was carefully prescribed, as was his brush. So was the timing of this act, and the reason for it. Nothing remarkable about the item but this: the stain on the wood once saved the life of every firstborn male inside the threshold that it marked.

When a twenty-something college student murders thirty-two of his peers on an ordinary April morning, the world snaps to and pays attention. The media seize on the story and run helter-skelter with it, offering an endless stream of coverage but scant explanation. Whatever motivating demons the young killer on the Virginia Tech campus harbored, he carried them unrevealed into one final, senseless murder—his own.

No one seemed to know much about the boy/man named Cho, who signed the roll of his freshman English class with a single, cryptic cipher: a question mark. We'll never know more, and we'll never know why. His thirty-two victims were silenced too—their barely discovered voices hushed too soon. So others talked instead. This is how we deal with death, with unmitigated disaster. We talk. And talk. And talk. We offer no explanations, just a steady stream of words and images. We want content and context, but finding very little of either, we simply babble on.

I watched some of this coverage after the Virginia Tech tragedy but found I could not watch for long. A network anchor asked a group of surviving students, "How will you look at these buildings and not be reminded of the carnage that happened here? Will Virginia Tech forever be synonymous with this murdering rampage?" What did she expect them to say? They were young. They were shocked to the core, trying to make sense out of senselessness. They said predictable things, of course. That the world would remember how they came together in solidarity in spite of their grief, how they demonstrated oneness and community. But it won't. Not really. It will remember the deaths that happened there, the lives cut short by a young man whose simmering rage finally spewed out in a sick and brutal rain of bullets.

When death trespasses in a supposedly safe place and innocent lives are lost, we scramble to make sense of the awful intrusion. We search for motive and meaning and reason. But here's the story that never gets told—at least not by CNN or NBC or FOX: We weren't made for death at all. We were made for life.

That's why death—any death, even one that arrives deep into old age and provides a blessed relief to sickness and pain—is always an affront, always a shock no matter how prepared for it we believe ourselves to be. Each of us has eternity infused into our souls beneath our bones and blood, and something in us knows it for a fact. We were made for never-ending, abundant life by a God who loves us and who went from heaven to earth and to hell and back to make sure we could have it.

The entire land of Egypt went to bed one night with sons they would not have when morning came. Death came calling and would not be denied. And this time God Himself was behind it. He'd fired nine warning shots across the bow of Pharaoh's royal court to prove His might on Israel's behalf. Bloody water. Frogs.

Gnats, flies, and dying livestock. Boils, hail, and locusts. Then darkness. And after the darkness—death.

Moses was witness to it all. Pharaoh rebuffed his every request to free the Israelites, even though it was clear that only Egyptians were suffering at the hands of Israel's God. But with the veil of darkness Pharaoh finally relented. For three days Egyptians sat in blackness too deep to move, but "all the sons of Israel had light in their dwellings" (Exodus 10:23). The ruler of Egypt summoned the shepherd of Israel's people and told Moses to go, with one caveat: "Only let your flocks and your herds be detained." Moses pressed him, saying: "You must also let us have sacrifices and burnt offerings, that we may sacrifice them to the LORD our God. Therefore, our livestock too shall go with us; not a hoof shall be left behind, for we shall take some of them to serve the LORD our God. And until we arrive there, we ourselves do not know with what we shall serve the LORD" (10:24–26).

But God hardened Pharaoh's heart, and he would not let them go. "Get out of my face!" he told Moses. "I've had it with you and your God." Then God announced to Moses His final, parting blow to Egypt: death to every firstborn in the land—from Pharaoh's palace to the slave girl's stable. "Pharaoh will not listen to you," God told Moses, "so that My wonders will be multiplied in the land of Egypt" (11:9).

For Egypt, God planned to execute a death sentence. No exceptions. No firstborn male, whether human or beast, would live.

But for Israel, He prescribed an odd means of protection from His own avenging wrath. It involved blood.

Take a lamb without blemish, He instructed the Israelites. One lamb for each household—a male, a year old. Then on the specified day, the whole assembly of the congregation of Israel was instructed to kill their lambs at twilight. "They shall take some of the blood and put it on the two doorposts and on the lintel of the houses in which they eat it" (12:7). They were to eat standing, with their shoes on and their belts fastened. Then, God told them, "I will go through the land of Egypt on that night, and will strike down all the firstborn in the land of Egypt, both man and beast; and against all the gods of Egypt I will execute judgments—I am the LORD. The blood shall be a sign for you on the houses where you live; and when I see the blood I will pass over you, and no plague will befall you to destroy you when I strike the land of Egypt" (12:12–13).

It happened just that way.

Pharaoh rose in the middle of the killing night, hearing the great outcry in his kingdom. His own son was dead. His servants' sons too. There was no house in Egypt where someone or some beast was not dead. But every firstborn of Israel with bloodstained doorposts lived. Pharaoh did not wait until morning to act. He called for Moses and Aaron in the middle of the night and instructed, "Rise up, get out from among my people, both you and the sons of Israel; and go, worship the LORD, as you have said. Take both your flocks and your herds, as you have said, and go, and bless me also" (12:31–32).

For 430 years Israel had lived in bondage to Egypt. And in a single night of death, they were set free. On that night death saw the blood and passed them over and broke the will of their enemy once and for all.

Death gets our attention. It got Pharaoh's attention. Thanks to Adam and Eve, it waits for all of us. Every firstborn Israelite spared on the night of the Passover was destined to die one day, as are we all. But God's great foreshadowing of the yearlings' blood on Jewish doorposts hinted that He would have the last word about death. His own Son would become the spotless lamb—His blood on a wooden cross would be our covering. He tasted death for those who place their faith in Him and left a roll of graveclothes behind as a testimony to His power over it.

In Jesus, death no longer has the last word.

Life never seems sweeter than when death lurks nearby. There's preciousness to every ordinary sneeze or sigh when we realize that even our sneezes and sighs are numbered.

In the last two years, death has sidled closer than I would wish, as my sister has battled cancer. I hate cancer. It is an enemy with no manners, no mercy, and no predictable pattern of attack. When my forty-nine-year-old, freckled, Scotch-Irish sister was diagnosed with a form that is more often seen in men than women, more frequently diagnosed in blacks than whites, and chiefly found among those over sixty rather than under it, she thanklessly beat each one of these statistical odds. "Couldn't I have just won the lottery?" she asked wryly, sitting in her hospital bed. Then to add to the already long shot, she was diagnosed with a rare accompanying condition that affects fewer than one in ten with her specific form of the disease.

This menacing threat to the extended good health of my best friend in the world has changed me in ways I am still discovering. I cannot begin to imagine how it has changed her. But I can say this: she is held. In Christ she has grown stronger by the day, even when her body has been at its weakest. She has gained a new vocabulary and mastered a new routine. She has adjusted to a new normal as she lives in the shadow of an incurable disease. She knows moments of fear and discouragement, but mostly she shines.

I have watched her meet with an amazing grace days of suffering that would have leveled me. I have seen her care for her own children's everyday ups and downs when she could hardly hold up her head. She has shown unfailing kindness to the endless parade of medical personnel dispassionately probing, poking, measuring, and medicating her. There have been dark days, and even a few desperate ones. She has learned a host of small skills she probably never aspired to perfect: giving herself injections, grocery shopping in an electric cart, drafting a durable power of attorney, and tying a mean head scarf, for starters. Even after treatments that her doctors have termed successful, she understands there are no guarantees.

Well, maybe one. We all go out of here the same way. She will die one day, and so will I. Maybe from cancer. Maybe from something else. Maybe soon. Maybe not for a long, long time. But death will not have the last word with her, or with me. We are covered with a blood that not only has defeated death but keeps on giving life to us each day. John Piper writes:

> For the Christian, eternal life has already begun and will not be interrupted by death or judgment. Jesus taught this when he said, "Truly, truly, I say to you, whoever hears my word and believes him who sent me has eternal life. He does not come into judgment, but has passed from death to life" (John 5:24 [ESV]). Already, by faith in Christ, our judgment is past and our death is past. Death is no longer death for those who are in Christ. The essence of what made it death has changed."[1]

Our penalty for sin has been paid. Our redemption from the curse of the Law is complete. The righteousness God requires has been provided for us. "Therefore," says Piper,

the sting of death is gone. Death is no longer the terror
that death used to be. Death is now a transition from
life to better life, from faith to seeing, from groaning
to glory, from good fellowship with Jesus to far better
fellowship with Jesus, from mixtures of pain and pleasure
to all pleasure, from struggles with sin to perfect affec-
tions for Jesus. We have [already] passed from death to
life.[2]

Take that, cancer. You're an awful bully, but you cannot win.

Like several million people in the late summer of 2007, I waited
anxiously to learn if Harry Potter would live or die in the seventh
and final installment of J. K. Rowling's megaselling series. I took
delivery of *Harry Potter and the Deathly Hallows* on a Friday—and
by Sunday (759 pages and three days later) I had my answer: Harry
did both. I imagine some folks think the subject matter of the
Harry Potter series (magic, wizards, spells, and the like) is unfitting
stuff for Christ-following readers. You may judge for yourself the
rightness of these stories, but *Deathly Hallows* was, for me, a great
adventure, and a well-told one at that.

In it, good and evil meet in a duel to the death. It looks as if
evil has won. Harry resolves to give his life to save the ones he loves.
"His job was to walk calmly into Death's welcoming arms."[3]

On the way to his final confrontation with evil, Harry is joined by a cloud of witnesses—those he loved most in life, all dead now. They have been where he is about to go. He asks if death will hurt. "Not at all," one of them answers. "Quicker and easier than falling asleep."[4] Then before he takes the last decisive step toward his end, he asks if these companions will stay with him. "Until the very end," his father promises.[5]

That promise is enough. Harry moves forward, and toward his certain death. It comes in a flash of green light as he faces evil head-on.

And then…he wakes. His wizarding mentor Dumbledore is there to greet him. Harry asks if he is dead. Dumbledore says he thinks not. "But I should have died," Harry protests. "I didn't defend myself! I meant to let him kill me!"[6]

And that willingness to be sacrificed, he discovers, has made all the difference.

We, too, have One who has tasted death for us. The writer of Hebrews says,

> In the days of his flesh, Jesus offered up prayers and supplications, with loud cries and tears, to him who was able to save him from death, and he was heard because of his reverence. Although he was a son, he learned obedience

through what he suffered. And being made perfect, he
became the source of eternal salvation to all who obey him,
being designated by God a high priest after the order of
Melchizedek" (5:7–10, ESV).

The perfect Son of God bled on wood, stretched out top to
bottom and side to side like the stained doorframe of the ancient
Jews' thresholds the night the death angel raided Egypt. He became our Passover lamb, offered once for all time:

> Every priest stands daily at his service, offering repeatedly
> the same sacrifices, which can never take away sins. But
> when Christ had offered for all time a single sacrifice for
> sins, he sat down at the right hand of God.... For by a
> single offering he has perfected for all time those who are
> being sanctified. (10:11–12, 14, ESV)

He did this not only so that death would be defeated, but so
that we might really live. Because the thief comes to kill and steal
and destroy. But Jesus came to give us life.

I wasn't surprised to read these words in Harry's story; they are
part of my story too: "The last enemy that shall be destroyed is
death."[7] It is from Saint Paul's first letter to the Corinthians, the fif-
teenth chapter:

As in Adam all die, so also in Christ shall all be made alive. But each in his own order: Christ the firstfruits, then at his coming those who belong to Christ. Then comes the end, when he delivers the kingdom to God the Father after destroying every rule and every authority and power. For he must reign until he has put all his enemies under his feet. The last enemy to be destroyed is death. (verses 22–26, ESV)

We are not immune from crazy shooters or tsunamis or terrorists or cancer—or even the indignities of chronic illness or the infirmities of old age. But they are toothless foes at best, because the blood on the wood says there's *more*.

"What's lost is nothing to what's found," says writer Frederick Buechner, "and all the death that ever was, set next to life, would scarcely fill a cup."[8]

I wish, oh how I wish, someone would rush to cover this story.

It is my eager expectation and hope that I will not be at all ashamed, but that with full courage now as always Christ will be honored in my body, whether by life or by death. For to me to live is Christ, and to die is gain.

—PHILIPPIANS 1:20–21, ESV

When this perishable will have put on the imperishable, and this mortal will have put on immortality, then will come about the saying that is written, "Death is swallowed up in victory. O death, where is your victory? O death, where is your sting?" The sting of death is sin, and the power of sin is the law; but thanks be to God, who gives us the victory through our Lord Jesus Christ.

—1 CORINTHIANS 15:54–57

7

A Golden Bell

The God of Show and Tell

From the blue and purple and scarlet yarns they made finely woven garments, for ministering in the Holy Place. They made the holy garments for Aaron, as the LORD had commanded Moses....

On the hem of the robe they made pomegranates of blue and purple and scarlet yarns and fine twined linen. They also made bells of pure gold, and put the bells between the pomegranates all around the hem of the robe, between the pomegranates—a bell and a pomegranate, a bell and a pomegranate around the hem of the robe for ministering, as the LORD had commanded Moses.

—EXODUS 39:1, 24–26, ESV

The bell is pure gold. Even tarnished, its beauty shines. So small that it is easily held between two fingers, it no longer makes a distinct sound. It was created to be one of many, a musical testimony to border the hem of a high priest's robe. Interspersed between the bells were fruitlike tassels—word and deed, word and deed, word and deed—to tell and show the glory and beauty of the one true God.

I grew up with a great big God. I first knew Him as the wonder-working God of Cecil B. DeMille's *The Ten Commandments:* the God who split seas in half and stood them upright, who created the heavens and the earth and ruled everything in between. As far as I was concerned, He majored in the grandest moments—stuff like Creation, the Flood, the plagues of the Exodus, pillars of cloud and fire, prophet-swallowing whales, and rock-wielding, giant-slaying shepherd boys. The miracles of the Gospels never seemed far-fetched to me; why shouldn't God the Son turn water to wine or multiply a few small fish and loaves to feed an overflow crowd? Why should healing sickness and raising the dead confound the awesome God of Abraham, Isaac, and Jacob? He was enormous, after all, bigger than any make-believe superhero and more powerful than any force of nature.

When I looked up at the nighttime stars, I easily imagined Him placing each one in its appointed course, and when I gazed by day at the clouds, it seemed reasonable to me that He shaped them with ease, the way I might have offhandedly molded Play-Doh at my schoolgirl desk. Nothing seemed too vast for my God's creative oversight. I was certain that He could handle anything.

Such a big God is a sure and steady comfort for a small child. But somehow along the road to maturity, I discovered that my big God had, in my mind at least, become a big-picture God—mighty, yes, but a divine doer who cared very little for the small things.

And nothing could be further from the truth.

The Israelites hadn't been long removed from bondage in Egypt when God laid down the law at Sinai. Having just seen Him accomplish amazing feats on their behalf, they were at least somewhat receptive to His newly spoken rules. But He didn't mean to oversee His people from some high and lofty perch above the desert. He meant to come close and to dwell nearby. He told their leader, Moses:

> Speak to the people of Israel, that they take for me a contribution. From every man whose heart moves him you shall receive the contribution for me. And this is the contribution that you shall receive from them: gold, silver, and bronze, blue and purple and scarlet yarns and fine twined linen, goats' hair, tanned rams' skins, goatskins, acacia wood, oil for the lamps, spices for the anointing oil and for the fragrant incense, onyx stones, and stones for setting, for the ephod and for the breastpiece. (Exodus 25:2–7, ESV)

It must have seemed, at first blush, a rather odd shopping list. The Israelites were, after all, a people on the move. They'd left Egypt in an awful hurry—but not before they had plundered the Egyptians of their gold, silver, and other riches. Now they could see why this extra cargo was given: God meant to make good use of it. And what, exactly, did the Almighty have in mind? "Let them make me a sanctuary," He said, "that I may dwell in their midst" (25:8, ESV). As Eugene Peterson so delightfully phrases it in The Message, God "moved into the neighborhood" (John 1:14). And not only did He have a particular neighborhood in mind—He had house plans drawn and was ready to build: "Exactly as I show you concerning the pattern of the tabernacle, and of all its furniture, so you shall make it" (25:9, ESV).

I have architect and designer friends who claim the worst possible client is one who has no idea what he or she wants. Let the record show that God would have made an excellent client. He knew exactly what sort of temporary home He was after, and He left virtually nothing to guesswork when He shared its design with Moses. He described the tabernacle or tent itself, with its eleven goats' hair curtains and fifty bronze clasps and upright frames of acacia wood. He specified its furniture, from the ark of the testimony and its mercy seat to the table and lampstand on down to its tableware—every single item specified. How much detail did God give? He described just the lampstand like this:

> The lampstand shall be made of hammered work: its base, its stem, its cups, its calyxes, and its flowers shall be of one piece with it. And there shall be six branches going out of its sides, three branches of the lampstand out of one side of it and three branches of the lampstand out of the other

side of it; three cups made like almond blossoms, each with
calyx and flower, on one branch, and three cups made like
almond blossoms, each with calyx and flower, on the other
branch—so for the six branches going out of the lampstand.
(25:31–33, ESV)

And *that* was just the lampstand itself—not its base or its
lampshades! All for the purpose that God Himself might draw near
and dwell among His people.

For those tending to the tabernacle—Moses's brother Aaron
as the high priest and his sons as priests—there were specific instructions for the very garments they would wear. From head to
toe their dress was ordered, down to the smallest, most elegant detail. A turban, a breastplate, shoulder pieces, a tunic, a sash, and a
robe were described, down to the very hem of that robe. There,
where the feet of the priests would stir up dust and where, no
doubt, the robe would trail in the blood of many sacrifices, a beautiful border was to be crafted.

And an odd one, at that.

Near the hem of the priests' robes, a row of richly embroidered
fruits—pomegranates—were interspersed with tiny golden bells
so that every movement of the priests' service would result in a brief
flash of color and the faint tinkling sound of music. It was dirty
work, theirs. But their service was a living, tangible show and tell
of distinct (if subtle) beauty.

Showing and telling. Standing in the gap. That was the priest's role. Showing forth the holiness and glory of God. Telling of His marvelous love and mighty works. And standing in the gap with a sacrifice for the people's sins that would be accepted by this holy God. Jesus, the ultimate high priest, did exactly this. He lived life on the edge—at the hem—between heaven and earth, and to this edge He brought words of truth and deeds (even small ones!) so beautiful and full of love that the world took notice. Ultimately He became the once-for-all sacrifice that His Father, God, required—giving Himself up on our behalf so that God could come near again.

> When Christ appeared as a high priest of the good things to come, He entered through the greater and more perfect tabernacle, not made with hands, that is to say, not of this creation; and not through the blood of goats and calves, but through His own blood, He entered the holy place once for all, having obtained eternal redemption. (Hebrews 9:11–12)

Those of us whom Christ has reconciled to God are priests too. Ours is the work of living on the edge between heaven and earth, and dressing that hem with a woven show and tell of word and deed—of truth and beauty—so that even in the smallest things, the world might see and be drawn nearer to God. We are, Peter said, "a chosen race, a royal priesthood, a holy nation, a people for his own possession, that you may proclaim the excellencies of him who called you out of darkness into his marvelous light" (1 Peter 2:9, ESV).

My proclaiming is mostly done in small, specific ways these days. I tell friends without joking that I feel "called to small." I don't aspire to stadium events, or the top of the *New York Times* bestseller list. I don't necessarily have what some call the gift of evangelism, but there's nothing I'd rather talk or write about than Jesus.

I'm not brave. I'm just in love.

So no one could have been more surprised than I was to find myself in a tiny town in Brazil called Boa Fe for the express purpose of sharing my faith, street by street and door by door, together with local missionaries and Brazilian translators. One evening, after a long day of walking and talking with my thirteen-year-old translator, Roosevelt, we stumbled on a group of boys playing a game of soccer in the dusty road. "Let's talk to them," Roosevelt prodded, obviously eager to practice his English-to-Portuguese-to-English skills. I hesitated. They were barefoot, shirtless, teenage boys—not an audience I'm exactly comfortable engaging. The hour was late, and I was tired.

"I'm not sure they'd like it if we interrupted their game," I said to my young friend. "Maybe we should just skip this one." Even before all the words were out of my mouth, I could see the disappointment on his face.

"Maybe you could just ask them for a minute of their time," I said, relenting. I had no idea what Roosevelt said to get their attention, but soon they were gathered around the two of us, looking at me as if I might have fallen from a tree. Roosevelt beamed a million-watt smile of encouragement at me, and I launched in. I only wanted a moment to tell them why I had come to Brazil, I said, and to tell them about my Lord Jesus and why I follow Him.

I spoke a sentence or two and then waited as Roosevelt translated. Truthfully, he might have been saying something entirely different from what I was cautiously speaking, but after a few sentences, I saw their faces soften. I told them that God loved them, that Jesus died to pay for their sins and give them life, and that I hoped they might decide to follow Jesus, as I had done long ago when I was young.

Before I knew it, I was squatting in the dirt with these boys, praying with them a prayer for their salvation. Do I know for sure that they understood what they were committing to? No. I don't. I can't. But I know that at that moment, the beauty and truth of the gospel met at the dusty, ragged hem of heaven and earth and swept me along for the ride. It was show-and-tell time in Boa Fe, and mysteriously, wondrously, God met us there in the road. A tiny moment. A ring of truth. An unlikely response. But a chance to proclaim His excellence at a juncture in time that would never come in the same way again.

"A bell and a pomegranate, a bell and a pomegranate, around the hem of the robe for ministering…" That's what God dictated His priestly servants should wear. He prescribed their attire down to the very hem—and then to its smallest detail. But the intricate tabernacle is no more. And the stunningly beautiful temple that replaced it is gone too. So where does the high priest minister today—and where do the bells of his robe ring out? The writer of Hebrews says, "The former priests were many in number, because they were prevented by death from continuing in office, but [Jesus Christ] holds his priesthood permanently, because he continues forever. Consequently, he is able to save to the uttermost those who draw near to God through him, since he always lives to make intercession for them" (7:23–25, ESV).

Jesus, our high priest, is at His Father's right hand, interceding inside the veil for us. And here, meanwhile, we minister in *His* name. In those places where heaven and earth approach each other, we live and move, and on our better days, our faith can be heard.

These ministering places are not necessarily mountaintops— or dusty roads half a world away from home. Mostly they're ordinary spaces infused with a holy hope. "Holy garments," said John Wesley, "were not made for men to sleep in, but to do service in, and then they are indeed for glory and beauty.… All true believers are spiritual priests.… And holiness to the Lord must be so written upon their foreheads, that all who converse with them may see they bear the image of God's holiness."[1]

Where do we find these ministering places? We don't, always. More often they find us. They are hidden in a song or a sigh, in sickness and in struggle. They are waiting in a day well spent, a job well done, a friend well loved. Perhaps we meet them in a kiss or a kind word—or on a good day, in both. They exist in memory tested and in muscle taxed. I can take the beautiful bells of my priestly robe, the winsome bells that whisper of Christ, to ball games and to book clubs, to baby-sitting gigs and Bible studies. They're small, these bells. They don't draw attention to me; they quietly, winsomely point to my great high priest: His beauty, His purity, His love.

A few years back I purchased a mostly blank book and a set of colored markers and set out to fill the book's pages with what could most easily be called desire. Or more appropriately, desires, plural. Like a kindergartner gone wild, I drew, scribbled, and made outrageously detailed lists of things I'd dreamed of, hoped for, but never dared say out loud to anyone. Only God knew these particular desires of my heart. He was the only one I trusted with them. I spilled out in fuchsia and blueberry ink a whole trove of hopes and wishes, and then I quietly put the book away.

So much time passed that I forgot having chronicled these things. In the course of a move, I found the self-made book, opened its cover, and began thumbing through its slightly faded pages. When I did, I discovered that God had remembered what I had forgotten—and that Jesus must have asked my heavenly Father to give me these desires He had long ago placed in my heart. Many had come to pass. Most of them without any help from me at all.

I had dreamed in vivid detail. (I drew pictures too.) A house with a porch swing. (Check.) A library with floor-to-ceiling shelves for books. (Check.) A horse. (Not yet.) A husband. (Not yet…and hopefully before the horse.) A place to regularly teach God's Word to women. (Check.) The chance to skydive. (Check.) See Paris. (Check.) Work barefoot. (Most days I do.) Publish a book in my own name. (Check, check, check, and check.)

As I ran my fingers over line after line, I could hardly contain the tears. God had literally given me the desires of my heart! He didn't just allow my wishes to come true; He placed the very desires deep in my heart that He meant to fulfill all along—to remind me of His love and to demonstrate to me His mighty power. For power and for glory, He ministered these sweet, specific graces to me. I did not merit them. He gave them anyway. To remind me that the plans He has for me are plans for welfare and not for calamity, to give me a future and a hope (see Jeremiah 29:11).

Turning each page, I could almost hear the tinkle of bells.

While I mean to stand at the edges for Jesus, ministering help and hope to a world desperate for both, He sits at the right hand of the Father and implores Him on my behalf, saying, "Father, would You bless her this way? And this way? She is Mine. I want to do her good."

He is showing and telling His great love both *to* me and *through* me. Do you see it?

Are there longings I am still waiting for His hand to fill? Yes, there are. But they pale (truly!) in comparison with what He has already done on my behalf. He knows me. He knows my heart. And He is not offended when I go all childlike on Him and hope wildly for good things—because He is a very good God. He welcomes my wanting. He embraces my need. Designs it, even. For my own good and for His great glory.

He remembers, even when I forget. Down to the smallest detail. I don't acknowledge Him enough as the grand architect He is—not only the designer of my so-great salvation but the shaper of a host of small, intricately extravagant graces as well.

How could I not love a bell-ringing, show-and-tell God like that?

> And the Word became flesh and dwelt among us, and
> we have seen his glory, glory as of the only Son from the
> Father, full of grace and truth.
>
> —JOHN 1:14, ESV

8

A Scarlet Cord

The God Who Includes

"Behold, when we come into the land, you shall tie this scarlet cord in the window through which you let us down, and you shall gather into your house your father and mother, your brothers, and all your father's household. Then if anyone goes out of the doors of your house into the street, his blood shall be on his own head, and we shall be guiltless. But if a hand is laid on anyone who is with you in the house, his blood shall be on our head…." And she said, "According to your words, so be it." Then she sent them away, and they departed. And she tied the scarlet cord in the window.

—JOSHUA 2:18–19, 21, ESV

It might have held a woman's hair in place or cinched her robe around her waist. This cord is wound into a neat little nest of solid red, still usable and strong. It once served as a sign of belonging and purchased the lives of those who hung it out for all to see. Who would have thought a cord of red could offer more protection than an army or bind so many strangers into one odd family?

The playground is not a democracy where all kids are created equal. When captains are named and teams selected, those who are most athletically gifted—the fastest runners, the sharpest shooters, the keenest passers—are snapped up first. The less quick or nimble are left to languish at the bottom of the draft barrel, waiting for the captain to call their names with a resigned sigh or an unenthusiastic shrug. Anyone who's been picked next to last knows the sting of grudging inclusion. Anyone whose name was routinely called first can remember reveling in the satisfaction of being among the most wanted.

Let the record show they never picked me first for softball. I was soundly average in any athletic contest—not the worst but certainly not among the best. My friend Cindy was the fastest of us all. She could outrun any girl and most of the boys. Sheri was the strongest. If you were hit by her throw in dodge ball, you would see the bruise for weeks, and she rarely missed her target. Team captains almost always called these two girls as their top picks. Winning was the object, and the odds decidedly improved with either of these girls on your team. On the playground they had the right stuff. They were included.

The harsh realities of playground politics proved reliable preparation for life. In theory we may all be created equal, but in fact it is our differences that most often mark us for selection or rejection. Smart people are chosen for scholarships or advanced study groups. The academically challenged need not apply. Socially adept, well-spoken individuals become class presidents or state representatives. Stutterers, not so much. I have yet to see a gawky, chubby-kneed brunette wear the Miss America crown. Step to the back of the line, please.

For good or for ill, we're judged—and included or not—based on criteria over which we have little or no control. Every one of us knows, in one way or another, what it is like to be on the fringes of some group, marginalized or maybe even ignored because of our differences. From the playground to the classroom, and from the clubroom to the boardroom, the unspoken question is, "Who belongs?" Who belongs on the ballot? Who belongs around the conference table? Who belongs in the Bible study, or the breakfast club, or the baby-sitting co-op? Too often the default answer is this: "Whoever is most like me."

I grew up in the suburbs of Houston, Texas, in the late '60s and '70s. All my friends were from my immediate neighborhood or my school. Our yards were the same size. Our houses looked alike. Our fathers had interchangeable jobs: draftsman, salesman, accountant. Our mothers mostly stayed at home. Our families drove American-made sedans or station wagons. We all owned a pet or two and had a sibling or two, seldom more. From elementary school through high school, I can remember only a handful of peers whose skin color or cultural experiences differed radically from mine. Racial segregation officially ended in the South with the Civil

Rights Act of 1964, but the world of my childhood was decidedly homogenous. Even in church.

Early on, God chose for Himself a people. The Jews, beginning with the patriarch Abraham, were the kin He set His sights on, and He meant to bless the world through them. Inclusion in God's family was not strictly limited to Jews, however. Jehovah God had criteria, yes. But His selection process was firmly rooted in faith—not in ethnicity or language or skin color. That's how a Canaanite prostitute named Rahab came to be named in Matthew's listing of the ancestors of the Jewish Messiah, Jesus Christ, "the son of David, the son of Abraham" (1:1).

No nice words can accurately describe the livelihood of Rahab. This resident of Jericho made her living satisfying the lusts of men. Her business was trading skin for money. One day, two strangers appeared at her door. They weren't locals. (She would have known them if they were.) These men asked only for lodging, and she gave it, no questions asked—because "no questions asked" was her stock in trade. The two men she harbored were Israelite spies sent by Joshua to do reconnaissance in the Promised Land—land that God had already given Israel to possess. The men came in secret, but their mission was soon detected: "And it was told to the king of Jericho, 'Behold, men of Israel have come here tonight to search out the land'" (Joshua 2:2, ESV). The king suspected that Rahab, given both her profession and the proximity of her dwelling to the city's gate, might well have seen them, so he sent a message demanding that she bring them out.

She didn't.

Instead, she hid them on her roof and sent the king's men on a fool's errand, saying, "True, the men came to me, but I did not know where they were from. And when the gate was about to be closed at dark, the men went out. I do not know where the men went. Pursue them quickly, for you will overtake them" (2:4–5, ESV).

Why did she deceive her own king to act on behalf of two strangers? "I know that the LORD has given you the land," she told them, "and that the fear of you has fallen upon us, and that all the inhabitants of the land melt away before you. For we have heard how the LORD dried up the water of the Red Sea before you when you came out of Egypt, and what you did to the two kings of the Amorites who were beyond the Jordan, to Sihon and Og, whom you devoted to destruction" (2:9–10, ESV).

Then Rahab did something totally unexpected. She asked to be on their team, to be included among God's people. She professed their God to be "God in the heavens above and on the earth beneath" (2:11, ESV). And she cast her lot with them. In exchange for helping them escape, she requested their protection when they came again to invade Jericho. And she asked for a sign that would prove she had it. They agreed, saying, "Behold, when we come into the land, you shall tie this scarlet cord in the window through which you let us down," and promised that the cord would keep her and her household safe during the coming siege. "Then she sent them away, and they departed. And she tied the scarlet cord in the window" (2:18, 21, ESV).

One seven-day parade and a trumpet blast later, Jericho fell. No one survived but Rahab and her household. The cord of scarlet proved to be their deliverance. The spies kept their word. "The prostitute and her father's household and all who belonged to her, Joshua saved alive. And she has lived in Israel to this day, because she hid the messengers whom Joshua sent to spy out Jericho" (6:25, ESV). Rahab, the unlikely call girl–heroine of Jericho, was *in*.

I was probably in my teens before I realized that God was not a Baptist. Shortly thereafter, I discovered He wasn't constrained to being Protestant either, or white or English speaking. While Sunday-morning church may still be the most segregated hour in America, God's family is remarkably, beautifully diverse. Its members have but a single common denominator: His name is Jesus. "We're all migrating to the place where our father lives," writes singer Derek Webb, "'cause we married in to a family of immigrants." Our allegiance, he goes on to say, is not to any person or country but to "a king and a kingdom."[1]

The scarlet thread that declares our allegiance to that king and kingdom is belief in Jesus Christ, and no other. The key to inclusion in the family of God is nothing more and nothing less than a red thread of sacrifice—the blood of God's only Son applied to sinners of every imaginable ilk. "God," says John Piper, "is no respecter of persons in salvation or in damnation. The human race—and every ethnic group in it—are united in this great reality: we are all depraved and condemned. We are all lost in the woods together, sinking on the same boat, dying of the same disease.... If I am among God's elect, it is owing entirely to God's free grace, not my distinctives."[2]

Of all the places where we might feel embraced and included, shouldn't the church be first? But even there we're not immune from concerns about fitting in. For over twenty years, I averted those concerns by attending a church where everyone else looked a lot like me. Racially, socially, economically, and politically. Sure, I remained single while the majority of its members were married—but for us there was a large and active single-adult ministry where most were trying hard to change their less-than-favored marital status. And a good many did.

Cocooned in such a homogenous place, I was unlikely to encounter anyone whose demographics seriously challenged my comfort. But I was also unlikely to be stretched in any significant way or to have my own personal biases exposed or changed for good. I didn't deliberately seek a different kind of church family, but one found me.

A pastor I'd met while mentoring a troubled teenager helped and then befriended me. I had heard about his inner-city church but didn't become curious enough about it to attend for quite a while. One Sunday that changed. I don't remember why. What I do remember is looking around me at a congregation of one hundred or so souls who were black, white, Latino, and Asian; young, middle-aged, and elderly; dressed up, dressed down; married, unmarried; exuberant in their worship style and subdued in contemplative quiet. *This,* I thought, *is what heaven will be like.* We'll be different, but united in a single, overriding allegiance that will make our differences seem not distracting but lovely, rich, and true.

The worship service itself was a little rough around the edges—mikes popped and cues were missed; long pauses sometimes fell where words were expected instead. But within a year this crazy quilt of a church became my home. Today I teach a women's class that is broad in its age range, diverse in race, stage of life, and marital status, and an enormous blessing to me as a teacher. I learn from these women each week, and I am grateful for their fellowship and their love of—and hunger for—God's Word.

Perhaps the most important thing I've discovered is this: beneath our clothes, our skin, and our favorite props we're not so different, after all. We're a little unsure, a little afraid, all of us—but full of hope rightly placed in a strong Savior who has loved us beyond reason. He is our common ground. The apostle Paul put it like this: "Just as the body is one and has many members, and all the members of the body, though many, are one body, so it is with Christ. For in one Spirit we were all baptized into one body—Jews or Greeks, slaves or free—and all were made to drink of one Spirit.… Now you are the body of Christ and individually members of it" (1 Corinthians 12:12–13, 27, ESV). The body of Christ. What a beautiful name for the church.

I've been blessed to see this body manifest itself in many forms and in many places: In the Lower Church of St. Francis in Assisi, Italy, with brown-robed brothers singing their morning and evening prayers. In big-city arenas where thousands flock to hear the good news proclaimed. On a hillside in Brazil in a half-finished church where I sat with local villagers, crammed shoulder to shoulder into the half of the building that boasted a roof, while the summer rain fell in solid sheets behind the preacher's back as he spoke. And in a small village in Scotland, where, after the morning service in a tiny Presbyterian church, the organist invited a group of us visiting Yanks back into the small sanctuary and played for us a spirited rendition of "The Star-Spangled Banner" on an old pump organ, beaming all the while.

I've experienced the richness of the body of Christ at work in vacant lots and makeshift clinics, in hospital rooms and at backyard barbecues. I have seen brothers and sisters in Christ give the shoes on their feet and the shirts off their backs to those who needed both. And I've delighted in seeing, around my own dinner table, the faces of friends who would not agree with my political views, my taste in books, or my penchant for old hymns, but love and serve the same God I do. Jesus Christ is our common ground. In Him, we're all grafted into a big, multifaceted, diverse (and yes, occasionally dysfunctional) family.

A good friend of mine—a pastor—sometimes says with a shrug and a smile when "family" relations get a little challenging, "If it weren't for Jesus, there'd be no good reason to be a Christian." Pastor David Anderson insists that, in spite of our differences, it is grace that allows us to stand together when it would be easier to divide: "The diversities of giftedness, gender, race, class, perspectives and preferences may collide and even compete at times. Grace within relationships then becomes the oil that keeps the body working together toward the goal of unity while fending off division within the body of Christ."[3]

Rahab appears again in the New Testament after her surprise entry in Matthew's genealogy of Christ. The writer of Hebrews remembers her too, and neither minces words about her background nor downplays the faith that wove her forever into God's great story. "By faith the walls of Jericho fell down after they had been encircled for seven days. By faith Rahab the prostitute did not perish with those who were disobedient, because she had given a friendly welcome to the spies" (11:30–31, ESV). And not *that* kind of friendly welcome. Hers was a welcome that said, "News of your God has come before you, and I, for one, am in awe. I think that beginning today I'd like to be on your side—and cast my lot with Him."

Her faith meant more than just an internal shift of allegiance. It meant she would be starting over, with no livelihood (all her former customers were soon to perish), no shelter (her living quarters became rubble when God gave Jericho over to Israel), and no doubt a good deal of emotional baggage as well. But she trusted the God of Israel to save her and to save her family…and her faith in Him worked her deliverance.

It always happens just that way.

Rahab is my sister, and she is yours too. Whether you feel like an insider or an outsider, a commoner or a king, a gifted leader or a quiet follower, a cord of red has stitched us together for time and eternity. In Christ we are included: woven into one great, many-hued tapestry of grace, adopted by a family where the thing that matters most is not where we come from or what we've done but who we've believed and how we've followed.

Do you not know that the unrighteous will not inherit the kingdom of God? Do not be deceived: neither the sexually immoral, nor idolaters, nor adulterers, nor men who practice homosexuality, nor thieves, nor the greedy, nor drunkards, nor revilers, nor swindlers will inherit the kingdom of God. And such were some of you. But you were washed, you were sanctified, you were justified in the name of the Lord Jesus Christ and by the Spirit of our God.

—1 CORINTHIANS 6:9–11, ESV

For in Christ Jesus you are all sons of God, through faith. For as many of you as were baptized into Christ have put on Christ. There is neither Jew nor Greek, there is neither slave nor free, there is no male and female, for you are all one in Christ Jesus. And if you are Christ's, then you are Abraham's offspring, heirs according to promise.

—GALATIANS 3:26–29, ESV

Balaam's Riding Crop

The God Who Speaks

When the donkey saw the angel of the LORD, she lay down under Balaam. And Balaam's anger was kindled, and he struck the donkey with his staff. Then the LORD opened the mouth of the donkey, and she said to Balaam, "What have I done to you, that you have struck me these three times?" And Balaam said to the donkey, "Because you have made a fool of me. I wish I had a sword in my hand, for then I would kill you."…

Then the LORD opened the eyes of Balaam, and he saw the angel of the LORD standing in the way, with his drawn sword in his hand. And he bowed down and fell on his face.

—NUMBERS 22:27–29, 31, ESV

Shorter than a walking stick, this rod bears a sweat-stained ring where its owner's hand must have gripped it. A crack runs the length of it, as if it had been crushed by some unseen pressure, but it is not broken. The stick was a hand tool—that much seems certain. But what did it mark or move or signal? And who in his right mind could imagine the unlikely conversation it provoked?

I 've experienced only a handful of star sightings in my life. Once, on a tour of the Vatican Museum in Rome, I spotted one of the world's most famous Lutherans-turned-Episcopalian: Garrison Keillor, the host of Minnesota Public Radio's *A Prairie Home Companion.* Keillor's stature and distinctive looks make him hard to miss, but I nudged my touring companions, who were busy looking at art or tapestries or paintings, to point him out before he turned a corner and disappeared. A few years later, during a working vacation in Colorado, I attended a Sunday-morning service at tiny Aspen Chapel and was stunned to see actor Kevin Costner walk in with a tall, beautiful blonde shortly after the sermon had begun. (Not stunned that he was with a tall, beautiful blonde—stunned that he and I were in the same place on the same morning and that the place was church.) In my own hometown of Houston, Texas, I once held the door for Barbara Bush, wife of the forty-first president of the United States, as we entered a small neighborhood drugstore at the same time.

As exciting as these random star sightings seemed when they occurred, they are in no way my most treasured brushes with fame. The thing that seems most remarkable to me is not that I briefly shared a moment with Mr. Keillor, Mr. Costner, or Mrs. Bush but that the God of the universe freely shares His *heart* with me! I belong to a God who speaks to His children. Not just on once-in-a-blue-moon occasions, but in ordinary moments and on ordinary days. Our God is a communicating deity—He is always speaking—and no limits constrain the ways in which He does so.

A quick pass through the Old and New Testaments proves it. Ours is the God who spoke in a cloud on a mountain, from the fire of a burning bush, through a disembodied hand writing on a wall, in a rainbow, in a rushing wind, in a blinding light, through prophets, angels, and, yes, even a talking donkey. (A friend of mine likes to say that if the Almighty could speak through Balaam's ass, he's hopeful that God might use him to deliver a message too.)

God speaks in any way He chooses, but especially through His inspired, written Word. No other means of heavenly speech will ever contradict what God has *already* said in the pages of the Bible; it is the plumb line against which all other communication must be measured. Dallas Willard writes, "The Bible is a finite, written record of what saving truth the infinite, loving God has spoken, and it reliably fixes the boundaries of what he will ever say to humankind."[1] It is through the words of His book that we come to discern and know the myriad *other* ways in which God may speak.

The writer of Hebrews says that "the word of God is living and active, sharper than any two-edged sword, piercing to the division of soul and of spirit, of joints and of marrow, and discerning the thoughts and intentions of the heart" (4:12, ESV). In other words, His book packs both power *and* insight. The psalmist describes the law of the Lord as "perfect, reviving the soul...making wise the simple...rejoicing the heart...enlightening the eyes"

(19:7–8, ESV). We don't have to wonder what God has already said; He has spoken clearly to us in the pages of His Word!

He speaks through His created order too. "The heavens declare the glory of God," the same psalm insists, "and the sky above proclaims his handiwork. Day to day pours out speech, and night to night reveals knowledge. There is no speech, nor are there words, whose voice is not heard" (19:1–3, ESV). In its beauty and its power, creation tells the story of the One who crafted everything that is. Every bit of glory revealed in this world in which we live says something about its maker. And as a prophet of old was to learn, sometimes even the very creatures God has created speak up on His behalf.

Israel was on the move through the land of Canaan, destroying the resident armies of Arad, Sihon, and Og. Fearing that his own people would become the next domino to fall in Israel's path, Balak, the king of Moab, called upon the prophet Balaam to come and put a curse on Israel—for a fee, of course. When Balaam got Balak's summons, he delayed the king's messengers overnight, saying, "Spend the night here, and I will bring you back the answer the LORD gives me" (Numbers 22:8, NIV).

But God's answer to Balaam was a firm no. He was not to predict victory for the Moabites, nor to curse Israel, ever. The next morning he rightly refused their request…until the king upped the ante. So Balaam bought more time and inquired again of the Lord. "That night God came to Balaam and said, 'Since these men have come to summon you, go with them, but do only what I tell you'" (22:20, NIV).

So Balaam got up, saddled his donkey, and went off with the princes of Moab, although God was not particularly happy about his motives. Writer Frederick Buechner describes what happened on the way: "Balaam's ass sees an angel of the Lord barring the way with a drawn sword in his hand and thereupon lies down in the middle of the road with Balaam still on his back. When Balaam clobbers him over the head with a stick, the ass speaks out reproachfully in fluent Hebrew, and then Balaam sees the angel too."[2]

Balaam's donkey rebuked him—balking and speaking when it saw God's angel with a sword in hand, blocking the prophet's way. In this case, the donkey was a good deal smarter than its rider! God may have chosen an unorthodox way to get Balaam's attention—but it worked. After He opened the donkey's mouth, God opened the prophet's eyes. Balaam told the Moabite king he had no choice but to "speak only what God puts in my mouth" (22:38, NIV). Instead of the curses Balak had ordered up, Balaam spoke blessings over Israel, just as God commanded him to do. And just as Balaam had refused at first to listen to God's warning from his donkey, so Balak refused to listen to God's warning message delivered to him through this prophet-for-hire.

God was speaking all right. But just like today, His audience was a little hard of hearing.

I've never heard God speak audibly or received an urgent message from Him through a talking animal of any kind. But God often speaks through a still, small voice—promptings of His Spirit of conviction or direction or illumination. "Now we have received not the spirit of the world, but the Spirit who is from God, that we might understand the things freely given us by God," writes the apostle Paul (1 Corinthians 2:12, ESV). I have heard this still, small Spirit voice—and disregarded it more than once.

Some years ago a woman I had known in college was kidnapped by rebel guerrillas while she was working as a medical missionary in Mozambique. I heard the news of her capture on the radio and, along with many others, hoped and prayed that her life would somehow be spared and she would return home safely. One afternoon at work I took a short break and went to a quiet place to pray for this friend. I bowed my head and took a deep breath. Almost as soon as my eyes closed, I heard this clear—although not audible—instruction: *Her feet. Pray for her feet.* It sounded ridiculous. I tried to ignore the thought. Why in the world would I pray about her feet? Her very life was at stake! As I tried again to focus, the words rushed back at me: *Her feet. Pray for her feet.* This happened several

times, and finally I resigned myself to pray for this woman's feet—
even though I felt ridiculous—just so I could get past the road-
block and move on to more important intercessory concerns.

"God," I said, "I don't know why I'm asking, but please take
care of her feet." Then I simply whispered several times, "I pray for
her feet; I pray for her feet." Nothing more came. I felt as though
my prayer time had been wasted, and I chastised myself for my in-
ability to execute even a brief, meaningful prayer of intercession
without my mind wandering.

Weeks later, her captors released this woman. She and her colleagues were all safe, and she returned home to the United States.
One Sunday evening she spoke of her experience at our church. I
was happy to see her looking thin but well. The enormous sanctuary was packed with people who had come to see her, and emotions
ran high. As she told her story, I was stunned to hear her say that
she and her fellow workers had been "force marched" through the
jungle at gunpoint for many days. "After the first few days," she
said, "the tennis shoes that I was wearing fell apart." Instantly I remembered: *Her feet. Pray for her feet.*

If I could have crawled off my pew in that moment and laid
facedown on the floor without calling attention to myself, I would
have. The instructions I had heard from that still, small (but insistent) voice weeks before now made perfect sense. God knew
He would spare her life. He wasn't asking me to pray for her life;
He was asking me to pray for her feet. And I was grateful I had,

even though I had done so grudgingly, completely ignorant of the reason why. As I remembered the insistent, silent voice of the Spirit virtually hijacking my prayers, I imagined an invisible army of intercessors—each with a different assignment—praying together for every need of this woman and her colleagues. My assignment, clearly, had been feet.

The apostle Paul also must have heard the still, silent voice to have written: "The Spirit helps us in our weakness. For we do not know what to pray for as we ought, but the Spirit himself intercedes for us with groanings too deep for words" (Romans 8:26, ESV). Now when the Spirit prompts me with words I can neither understand nor ignore, I pray them. It is enough to have heard Him speak. I do not have to understand.

Could anyone have been more surprised than Balaam to hear his own donkey rebuke him with a human voice? After all, he'd billed himself as a prophet—a mouthpiece of God—but instead of using a prophet to get his point across to the paying customers, God chose to send a word *to* Balaam through the mouth of the dumb animal he was riding on!

When God wants to get our attention, He is not limited in the ways He can do so.

He may speak through His Word…or His prophets or preachers or teachers. He may speak through creation—the very stuff of heaven and earth. Or He might speak strongly but inaudibly straight to the human heart. No matter how the message comes, it comes with utter authority. God may whisper at times—but He does not stutter.

"Within the lines or in between the lines," says author Ken Gire, "God may be speaking. Every book we read, every movie we see, every person we talk with, every song we listen to, every moment in our lives, in fact, should be subjects for reflection and could be ways through which God is speaking."[3]

What about old Balaam? Was he dense? Hardhearted? Not paying attention or not expecting to hear from the God for whom he claimed to be a spokesman? The prophet struck his donkey three times before it turned and spoke to him. Three times an angel stood before the animal with a sword drawn in his hand. The first time the donkey saw the armed angel, it turned out of the road and went into an open field. Balaam struck the donkey sharply and steered it back into the road. The second time it was hemmed in with a wall on either side, and with no place to turn, it pressed into one wall, crushing Balaam's foot against it. So he struck it again. The third time, with no way to turn either to the right or left, the donkey lay down in the road and simply refused to move. Balaam was angry. He struck it with his staff.

"What have I done to you," the donkey said, "that you have struck me these three times?… Am I not your donkey, on which you have ridden all your life long to this day? Is it my habit to treat you this way?" (Numbers 22:28, 30, ESV).

"No," said Balaam. He couldn't remember anything like this happening before.

Then God opened his eyes, and he saw what the donkey had already seen: an angel of God ready to strike him down if he had not halted in his path. Balaam fell on his face, heard the angel say he meant to kill him, and then confessed: "I have sinned, for I did not know that you stood in the road against me. Now therefore, if it is evil in your sight, I will turn back" (22:34, ESV).

Repentance is an excellent response to the warning voice of God. And obedience to His commands is like sweet music to His ears. "Go with the men, but speak only the word that I tell you," the angel instructed (22:35, ESV). And Balaam, listening now as if his life depended on it, did just that.

I want to hear from God. I do. But even though I know He speaks, I sometimes miss His words. I forget to live expectantly—on tiptoe—believing that He has something to say to me…and that He means to do so. If it's true that we see what we are looking for, then we hear, too, what we are listening for. If I don't hear His voice, it's probably not because He is silent but because I've failed to listen for Him. I simply don't expect Him to speak.

But there's more. Even if I do anticipate that God will speak to me—through His Word, through people, through His creation, through His Spirit, or just through everyday life—I must be able to discern that it is *His* voice I am hearing. And this takes time. I may have trouble recognizing the voice of someone I've only met casually. But if we have spoken at length, spent time in each other's presence, and especially if we have shared intimate details of our lives with each other—I *will* know my friend's voice. My closest friends and family don't announce their names when they call. They don't need to. I recognize them at the sound of their first word. Jesus said those who are His know His voice too:

> He who enters by the door is the shepherd of the sheep.
> To him the gatekeeper opens. The sheep hear his voice, and
> he calls his own sheep by name and leads them out. When
> he has brought out all his own, he goes before them, and
> the sheep follow him, for they know his voice....
>
> I am the good shepherd. I know my own and my own
> know me, just as the Father knows me and I know the
> Father; and I lay down my life for the sheep. (John 10:2–4,
> 14–15, ESV)

I first heard His voice as a child. He drew me to Himself when I was only a girl, but I knew—I knew!—that I had heard the irresistible voice I would follow for life. He is indeed my Shepherd.

He leads me in and out, and although I have more than once exercised a sheep's stubborn tendency to wander, He has consistently and clearly called me back. Every time. We have history, He and I, and I have followed Him long enough to know that no other voice can compel me as His does.

Here's what I know about my Shepherd's voice: It will never deceive me. It will never endanger me. It will never tempt me to sin or tell me a lie. It will never mock me or shame me or condemn me, even when it breaks my heart by telling me the truth about my sin. It will not trick me or taunt me or compare me to another. And it will never send me away. Ever.

Is it any wonder I long to hear from Him?

This ever-speaking God saved His best word for last. Singer and songwriter Michael Card says, "He spoke the incarnation and then so was born the Son. His final word was Jesus, He needed no other one."[4] The writer of Hebrews put it this way: "Long ago, at many times and in many ways, God spoke to our fathers by the prophets, but in these last days he has spoken to us by his Son, whom he appointed the heir of all things, through whom also he created the world" (1:1–2, ESV). And the apostle John added his testimony as well: "The Word," he said, "became flesh and dwelt among us, and we have seen his glory, glory as of the only Son from the Father, full of grace and truth" (John 1:14, ESV).

All that God would say to us today is wrapped up in the person of Christ Himself—God in the flesh, God made man. Jesus Christ is the fully formed embodiment of God's every communication to us. He is not words but the very Word itself!

I love words. I always have. I love reading them. Writing them. Hearing them spoken and sung. I'm intoxicated by their combinations in poetry and lyrics and psalms and stories. I collect them in my bookshelves and write them on my walls. So I marvel at this reality: that "God spoke, and the Word—all that he is—became flesh. The story he had written out of time came into time and unfolded before the very eyes of its audience. The Word became flesh, and the story came to life. With one word—Jesus—God-the-author embodied redemption and revelation all at once and for always. With one Word he pierced the darkness, paid the ransom, split the veil, and ran toward the prodigal on his dusty, desperate road home. Just a single word."[5] Jesus. There is nothing more to say.

He who comes from above is above all. He who is of the earth belongs to the earth and speaks in an earthly way. He who comes from heaven is above all. He bears witness to what he has seen and heard, yet no one receives his testimony. Whoever receives his testimony sets his seal to this, that God is true.

—JOHN 3:31–33, ESV

The Mighty One, God, the LORD, has spoken,
And summoned the earth from the rising of the sun
   to its setting.

—PSALM 50:1

My sheep hear My voice, and I know them, and they
follow Me.

—JOHN 10:27

A Head of Barley

The God Who Gleans Joy from Sorrow

At mealtime Boaz said to her, "Come here and eat some bread and dip your morsel in the wine." So she sat beside the reapers, and he passed to her roasted grain. And she ate until she was satisfied, and she had some left over. When she rose to glean, Boaz instructed his young men, saying, "Let her glean even among the sheaves, and do not reproach her. And also pull out some from the bundles for her and leave it for her to glean, and do not rebuke her."

—RUTH 2:14–16, ESV

Long, grasslike strands shelter the tiny kerneled rows inside this head of grain. Barley was an early crop, harvested well before the others—a multipurpose food, and common. The kernels in the head itself resemble the tight braid of a woman's hair: symmetrical, neat, even. Gleaned by a hungry widow with an uncertain future, this scrap came from the field of a generous kinsman and somehow wove two fragmented lives into the promise of life-giving, uncommon bread.

A Word document I was drafting prompted me to "Type a question for help." Just for fun, I typed, "How can I understand?" Microsoft Office Online quickly offered a plethora of options: analyzing sales opportunities for risk, evaluating life/work benefits, planning your channel strategy (I wasn't sure I had one), learning how to speak to a computer, tracking and reporting organizational changes, creating a great team environment, communicating budget data to management, tracking your direct-mail campaign, securing legal documents and files, and many more. I resisted the temptation to type this follow-up question: "Huh?"

It seems the good programmers both overestimated my intelligence and underestimated the scope of my problem. There are simply too many things in life I don't understand but would like to…and I'm not sure if an adequate Help function exists for my dilemma.

How can I begin to understand cancer's mean assault on one treasured life after another? Or the reluctance of believing friends to work toward a common goal, then, once persuaded about the goal, their disagreeing on how to get there? What sense can be made of bridges that crumble at rush hour or of a young baseball coach struck dead in an instant by an errant foul ball? How can I comprehend the tortured unraveling of a marriage between two good people? As much as I try to, I cannot. And it's not just other people's dilemmas that baffle me. My own do too. I don't understand why longtime friendships fizzle when life circumstances change, why colleagues compete as if only one of us could be happy or successful, or even why I am kinder at times to strangers than I am to the people I love best.

The Help feature on my computer offers no real remedy for these things. A mathematically constructed, logical algorithm cannot provide the sort of solutions I am looking for. Its answers speak to my head. But I am asking with my heart, *When the world is not right, how can I understand?*

I've read the best-selling books that promise I can have an absolutely stellar life now, or change my relationships for the good in ten days or ten steps or even ten minutes. I just don't buy it. And the implication that the right amount of faith in God will make me an instant victor I find almost insulting. Good people do suffer. I suffer at times too. There are some losses that simply cannot be explained. It's almost as if God speaks a higher language than the one I use to form my questions—and that my failure to understand His answers is *precisely* the point at which my faith begins to stretch and grow.

I wonder if God's answer to "How can I understand?" might be simply, "You cannot. But I do." And I wonder when I will ever learn that this could, in fact, be more than enough.

I'm sure Naomi did not understand. She'd left her home in Bethlehem of Judah when a famine struck the land and moved with her husband, Elimelech, and their two sons to the pagan country of Moab. She left Bethlehem—the city whose very name means "house of bread"—due to lack of bread. But Elimelech died in Moab, leaving her a widow with two sons, and these sons married Moabite wives. Ten years later both men died, neither of them having fathered a child. Now Naomi was a mother-in-law to two foreign daughters-in-law, with no heirs in sight. She was far from home and all alone, with no good prospects for a future.

She had heard a rumor in Moab, however, that the Lord had visited His people back in Judah and given them food. So she decided to return home. (Better to beg for bread in your homeland than in the land of strangers.) Her daughters-in-law prepared to go with her, but she strongly discouraged them: "Go, return each of you to her mother's house. May the LORD deal kindly with you as you have dealt with the dead and with me. May the LORD grant that you may find rest, each in the house of her husband" (Ruth 1:8–9).

They did not want to leave her, but Naomi insisted, saying she had nothing to offer them: no more sons and no more hope: "Would you therefore refrain from marrying? No, my daughters; for it is harder for me than for you, for the hand of the LORD has gone forth against me" (1:13).

The younger women wept, and one of them—Orpah—did turn back. But the other daughter-in-law, named Ruth, refused. "Do not urge me to leave you or turn back from following you," she pleaded, "for where you go, I will go, and where you lodge, I will lodge. Your people shall be my people, and your God, my God" (1:16).

Ruth acknowledged what Naomi could not yet see: that even in the worst of times, God was worth following. There is nothing contradictory (even though we hope there might be) in claiming both that God is sovereign and that He has "gone forth against [us]." Job said it: "The LORD gave and the LORD has taken away. Blessed be the name of the LORD" and "Though He slay me, I will hope in Him" (Job 1:21; 13:15). David said it: "My God, my God, why have you forsaken me? Why are you so far from saving me, from the words of my groaning?" (Psalm 22:1, ESV). Even the Son of God echoed the words of David's psalm as He hung dying on the cross!

Sometimes God wounds us before we are blessed. John Piper says of the sovereign working of God: "He gives rain and he takes rain. He gives life and he takes life. In him we live and move and have our being. Nothing—from a toothpick to the Taj Mahal—is rightly understood except in relation to God. He is the all-encompassing, all-pervading reality."[1]

In other words, in blessing or in pain, God rules.

I would prefer to choose my suffering as an elective, but God seems to consider it a prerequisite course. "Count it all joy, my brothers," writes James, "when you meet trials of various kinds, for you know that the testing of your faith produces steadfastness" (James 1:2–3, ESV). James seems certain that trials will come to us. He doesn't say "if" but "when." Even so, when my "trials of various kinds" arrive, I view them like a plate set before me bearing someone else's unappetizing dinner: "Why are You bringing me *this*? I ordered the life of ease."

God is unfazed. If my life is a story He is writing (and I believe it is), conflict is sure to come. It is the fuel of the plot—not an aberration. In God's authorial sovereignty, every trial and every struggle contribute in a unique way to the richness of the story and build to its desired climax and conclusion.

Hollywood screenwriting coach Robert McKee teaches would-be screenwriters how to craft stories that will grab the heart of an audience and run away with it. He claims that nothing moves forward in a story except through conflict. He insists—and he should know—that conflict lies at the heart of every true, compelling, and beautiful story. "Conflict is to storytelling," says McKee, "what sound is to music."[2]

Each inevitable conflict bears its own temptation. When the plot of our story thickens, we are tempted to resist and employ do-it-yourself fixes. One fix might be denial. We can simply deny our trouble, pretending it does not exist. We can insist that our life is going along perfectly well, thank you very much, and that we never, ever struggle. Or we can oversimplify. We can dumb down our struggle and maintain that the plot of our story is really very simple: "Jesus loves me, this I know." And Jesus does. But to say that our story is no more complex than a single fact is simply not true. "And they lived happily ever after" is not a story. What comes before this hoped-for sentence is what makes the story. We may even be tempted to manipulate our story by deciding in advance where it is headed, editing out every seemingly dissonant scene or bit of dialogue. Or we can despair, as Naomi did, believing that all is lost when confusion or heartbreak pulls us up short.

Why doesn't this kind of denial, editing, or plot oversimplification work? Well, it might—if what we desire more than anything is a boring, unengaged, toothless, flat-line kind of existence. But we were made for no such tale. We were made for an abundant, soul-satisfying, God-glorifying story of a life, one that brings God praise and brings us joy. And He weaves it line by masterful line, sometimes crafting lines that hurt before they bless.

So what does a God lover do when God does not seem to be acting in a loving way? when she does not understand? She keeps loving. Trials for the godless are just that: trials, nothing more. But for the godly, trials are tests of our faith and opportunities for strengthening it. God's sovereignty isn't always soft, but His goodness and mercy endure. The pain of our past does not mean that no hope exists for the future. This kind of trusting love is costly, but the alternatives always cost us more.

Back home in Bethlehem, Naomi and Ruth faced a challenge. They had to eat. The famine had ended, but no welcome committee rushed to deliver loaves of freshly baked bread to their door. They were two widowed women in a patriarchal society, with no man to keep them from starving or to protect them from being preyed upon.

The painful years in Moab must have etched themselves on Naomi's face, for at first her women friends did not recognize her. "Is this Naomi?" they asked, uncertain that it could be the woman they remembered. She quickly set them straight: "Do not call me Naomi; call me Mara [bitter], for the Almighty has dealt very bitterly with me." In case they wondered what she might mean, she elaborated: "I went out full, but the LORD has brought me back empty. Why do you call me Naomi, since the LORD has witnessed against me and the Almighty has afflicted me?" (Ruth 1:19–21).

But the writer of Naomi's story inserts this small footnote with regard to the divine timing of their return: "And they came to Bethlehem at the beginning of barley harvest" (1:22).

Two more facts come to the forefront of the story soon after their return. A distant relative of Naomi's deceased husband, a man named Boaz, lived in Bethlehem and had fields of grain. And the law provided both for the poor to glean in the fields after the harvest and for a kinsman to redeem the property of a less-fortunate relative. Both of these laws were deeply woven into Naomi's story of redemption, even though she did not know it.

As Providence would have it, Ruth set out to glean—and "happened to come to the portion of the field belonging to Boaz, who was of the family of Elimelech" (2:3). Ruth soon caught the eye of Boaz, who asked the foreman of his harvesters, "Whose young woman is this?" (2:5). The foreman told Boaz as much as he knew: that the woman was a foreigner named Ruth, who had come from Moab with her mother-in-law, a widow named Naomi. The foreman then added his own two cents, saying, "She said, 'Please let me glean and gather after the reapers among the sheaves.' Thus she came and has remained from the morning until now; she has been sitting in the house for a little while" (2:7).

Then in an act that went against culture and custom, Boaz addressed Ruth directly. "Listen carefully, my daughter," he said. "Do not go to glean in another field; furthermore, do not go on from this one, but stay here with my maids. Let your eyes be on the field which they reap, and go after them. Indeed, I have commanded the servants not to touch you. When you are thirsty, go to the water jars and drink from what the servants draw" (2:8–9).

Amazing! He told her to stay in his fields, and he promised her productivity and protection there. Yet Ruth was a nobody. A foreigner. A widow with nothing to her name but another widow to feed.

She "happened" to come to the portion of the field belonging to a member of her deceased father-in-law's family. This man "happened" to notice her and took pains to protect her. His kindness did more than impress her. It literally bowled her over—bending her low to the ground in a gesture of humility and respect for the man whose goodness she could not understand. "Why have I found favor in your sight…," she asked him, "since I am a foreigner?" (2:10). She must have been surprised at his answer and at what he knew of her: "All that you have done for your mother-in-law after the death of your husband has been fully reported to me, and how you left your father and your mother and the land of your birth, and came to a people that you did not previously know. May the LORD reward your work, and your wages be full from the LORD, the God of Israel, under whose wings you have come to seek refuge" (2:11–12).

Later, at mealtime, Boaz invited Ruth to share his table and his bread and wine and roasted grain. So she sat among his employees—not as a beggar!—and ate until she was satisfied, with food to spare. When Ruth returned to the field, Boaz ordered his reapers to purposely pull out sheaves from their sacks and leave them on the ground for Ruth to glean. Her efforts by the end of the day resulted in a harvest of more than half a bushel of grain, which she brought home to Naomi, along with her leftovers from lunch. Then she told her mother-in-law the story of the kind man in whose field she had worked…a man whose name was Boaz.

I wonder if Naomi might have smiled then, for the first time since her husband's death. Surely she could see the fingerprints of God in her daughter-in-law's story. "May he be blessed by the LORD," she exclaimed, "who has not withdrawn his kindness to the living and to the dead" (2:20). Then she told Ruth that Boaz was a close relative, "one of our redeemers" (2:20, ESV). I can almost see her clapping her hands together in the joy that they had not been forgotten. And then Naomi hatched a plan. "People who feel like victims," says John Piper, "don't make plans. As long as Naomi was oppressed; as long as she could only say, 'The Almighty has dealt very bitterly with me,' she conceived no strategy for the future.... Strategies of righteousness are the overflow of hope."[3]

Naomi's plan was for Ruth to present herself to Boaz in a private place and ask for his "covering" as a kinsman and redeemer. It was risky. It was bold. And Boaz acted righteously, doing everything in his power to protect Ruth's innocence and uphold the law. To demonstrate his desire to do good to her, Boaz sent Ruth away with six measures of barley to share with Naomi. She saw it as a good sign, and it was. Boaz did redeem all that belonged to his relative Elimelech—and took Ruth to be his wife.

If the story had ended there, it would have been rich and beautiful enough. But there is more. Ruth the Moabite gave birth to a son by Boaz—a son she laid in the arms of Naomi, a sweet and unexpected blessing after all the pain of her past. And then...the baby boy they named Obed became the father of Jesse. And Jesse was the father of David. And generations later, from the house of David, in the city of Bethlehem, another child was born: "a Savior, who is Christ the Lord" (Luke 2:11). This tragic story of loss turned from bitter to sweet with a few gathered bits of grain, and as a result, the One who called Himself the bread of life was born in the "house of bread."

The redemptive goodness and beauty and truth born out of Naomi's awful struggle leave me breathless but satisfied. And encouraged. Her sad-to-sweet story helps me to believe that, out of my own conflicts and from the very things that I need help to understand, God is doing good for me. My life begins to change when I cease to deny or simplify its conflicts, choosing instead to receive what God gives—and trusting in His redemptive power to make from my trials something God-honoring and good.

My own story has had plenty of harrowing twists and turns and, like Ruth's and Naomi's, has included things I neither ordered nor expected. But He has been with me, and He has been true. When I don't understand, He is working. When my heart is broken, He is moving to bless me once more. When the future looks bleak, He has not lost heart—and neither should you and I. He has proven that there is enough hope in the tiniest bit of grain to get us safely home.

I have been young and now I am old,
    Yet I have not seen the righteous forsaken
    Or his descendants begging bread.
All day long he is gracious and lends,
    And his descendants are a blessing.
                —Psalm 37:25–26

What then shall we say to these things? If God is for us,
who can be against us? He who did not spare his own
Son but gave him up for us all, how will he not also with
him graciously give us all things?
                —Romans 8:31–32, esv

A Shepherd's Harp String

The God of the Little Guy

The LORD said to Samuel, "How long will you grieve over Saul, since I have rejected him from being king over Israel? Fill your horn with oil, and go. I will send you to Jesse the Bethlehemite, for I have provided for myself a king among his sons."…

When they came, he looked on Eliab and thought, "Surely the LORD's anointed is before him." But the LORD said to Samuel, "Do not look on his appearance or on the height of his stature, because I have rejected him. For the LORD sees not as man sees: man looks on the outward appearance, but the LORD looks on the heart."

—1 SAMUEL 16:1, 6–7, ESV

The string lies soundless, no hint of the music that once hummed and vibrated through it. Loose, not taut, it coils around the other items near it. Other strings, four or eight or even ten more, once combined with this one to make an iPod for an ancient shepherd, loaded only with the music he carried in his heart. They say this shepherd even played for his enemy on request.

*O*nce a year I attend an international gathering of Christian retailers: publishers, writers, agents, publicists, booksellers, and others whose business is (chiefly) producing books that sell. I'm always a little overwhelmed by this event: there is simply too much activity in one place at one time for my comfort. Usually I stay only two or three days at most—enough time to make a few meetings, pick up some catalogs, and browse upcoming releases. It amuses me a little that I am given a nametag that screams AUTHOR in all caps, when, if you asked me what I do for a living, I would choose instead to say, "I write." Thankfully I am well under the radar here, not notable enough to cause a stir and well able to flip my nametag over and do a little anonymous people-watching myself.

Seeing writers interact with their world apart from the printed page is a fascinating thing, and book signings always provide a fine opportunity to do just that. Some authors travel with "horse holders": people who carry their pens or water bottles, even open the pages of each book to be signed and place it in front of them in assembly-line fashion. These authors may either engage those who receive their autograph or else barely acknowledge their presence.

On my last trip to this event, I observed one nearly ninety-year-old teacher-writer-theologian (to call him an author seems almost a slight) arrive a mere five minutes late for his signing, apologizing in a soft British accent to the small handful of people waiting for him. "So sorry," he said settling into his chair. "I'm a little slow."

Then he removed the cap from his own pen, smiled at the first person in line, and reached inside his jacket for a decidedly untrendy pair of glasses. "I'm torn," this man said to her with a sheepish shrug. "If I put these on, my handwriting will look nicer, but I won't see your face as well." Then he began to slowly inscribe her name in the book, with much greater care than he wrote his own.

Another author, this one a third the age of the former, had signed a half-dozen books before he'd given the first one away. He simply signed each book, pushed it down to the end of the desk, and left it there to be picked up while he efficiently signed the next. He seemed quite confident that he had mastered a system for dealing with his public. He was organized, but not at all engaged. For him, it was clearly all about his book. But he did not seem to realize (or care) that for those standing before him, it was about the *moment*.

When Israel wanted a king, it was up to her prophets to listen for God's selection and then announce His decision. Their first king was straight from central casting: Saul was a strong, handsome man who stood head and shoulders above his countrymen. His daddy was rich, and he himself was brash and bold. God told the prophet Samuel: "About this time tomorrow I will send you a man from the land of Benjamin, and you shall anoint him to be prince over My people Israel; and he will deliver My people from the hand of the Philistines" (1 Samuel 9:16).

Saul did not rule for long over the Israelites before they began to regret ever having asked for a king at all. They said to Samuel, "Pray for your servants to the LORD your God, so that we may not die, for we have added to all our sins this evil by asking for ourselves a king" (12:19). Samuel assured the people that if they continued to serve the Lord with all their heart, He would bless them in spite of their ill-advised clamoring for a king. "For the LORD will not abandon His people on account of His great name," Samuel said, "because the LORD has been pleased to make you a people for Himself" (12:22).

Saul's rule lasted long enough for him to successfully wage war against the armies of the Moabites, the Ammonites, the Edomites, and the Philistines. "Wherever he turned," the Bible says, "he inflicted punishment" (14:47). But Saul had issues. His disobedience to God as commander in chief caused God to reject him as king. Again, the word came through Samuel: "I regret that I have made Saul king, for he has turned back from following Me and has not carried out My commands" (15:11). Although Saul confessed his disobedience, his time was up, and Samuel minced no words delivering God's message: "The LORD has torn the kingdom of Israel from you today and has given it to your neighbor, who is better than you" (15:28).

Israel's second king was a surprise to everyone, especially to the king himself. This time God dispatched Samuel to Bethlehem, to the house of Jesse, and promised, "I have selected a king for Myself among his sons" (16:1). When Samuel arrived, Jesse marched seven sons out before the prophet, who examined each one carefully before he announced with finality, "The LORD has not chosen these" (16:10). When asked if he had no other sons, Jesse offhandedly mentioned his youngest—a shepherd boy who liked to sing and play the harp in his spare time. "Send for him," said Samuel—and Jesse did (16:11, NIV). The boy's name was David, and he was the very antithesis of Saul. He was small and ruddy, with beautiful eyes. "This is he," God said (16:12).

And so David was anointed king—although Saul was painfully slow in relinquishing the throne. In fact, King David spent the first part of his reign either in the service of or on the run from his predecessor, who seemed to want nothing more than to kill young David and be done with it. As often as he could, when an evil spirit was upon Saul, David would take his harp and play it until his nemesis was refreshed and well again. It was an odd way for the greatest king of Israel to begin his assignment: he was called upon to serve before he was allowed to rule.

The day before I watched these authors sign their books, I heard a noted pastor-theologian speak on the topic "What are writers good for?" He concluded that writers (not authors) are good for tending to things, using revelatory language—and that their calling is to a slow process, not unlike spreading manure. "Manure is not a quick fix," he said. "It's the stuff of resurrection.... God is not in a hurry."[1]

His message was clear: for the true God-follower, successfully living out your faith is not about what you can make or conquer or sell—even if you are very good at all three. It's about those everyday moments in which you can obey and embody Christ and bring Him into each human interaction with an unselfconscious grace.

Two other moments from this particular conference remain fixed in memory. One afternoon I rode a hotel elevator with two women, neither of whom I knew. (They both had on nametags, but I didn't strain to read them while pretending not to.) We politely regarded one another and may have exchanged a word or two of small talk. When the first woman exited the elevator at the floor just below mine, the second woman turned to me and said, "That was the great _____ _____ you just rode the elevator with." I wasn't sure how to respond. When she said this woman's name, I recognized it, and you might too. I've read one of her books and enjoyed it; she has written dozens more, and they are very popular. But I wasn't sure what to say to such a reverential announcement. I simply nodded while I stifled the urge to reply, "Yes, and she just rode with us!"

The second incident took place in the lobby of the same hotel that evening as I waited for my dinner partner to arrive. The place was very busy, and just in front of me were several women who appeared to be friends. One of these was pushing a stroller occupied by a toddler who looked to be under the age of two and obviously had Down syndrome. As this group huddled to talk, a gaggle of people swept by, and at its whirling center was another writer whose name you might know. I had seen her sign books the day before, taking a moment or two with each person and speaking graciously to all. She had a laugh that was infectious; she seemed able to make those around her comfortable in her presence. When she spotted the little girl in the stroller, she stopped in her tracks with a delighted gasp, bent low in front of her, and did what nearly every woman does in the presence of a cute baby: she cooed and clucked and looked as if she could eat this little girl with a spoon. She asked her mother her name and how old her daughter was, and congratulated her on having such a precious gift in her possession. I wondered as I watched if it might have been one of the few times this scene had been played out for this particular mom. It wasn't fake. It wasn't forced. It was just a brief moment of delight, shared one woman to another. No cameras rolling. No one watching (except maybe me). I decided right then and there that whatever this woman wrote next, I was reading it.

God seems to enjoy confounding us by His choices. He exalts the humble and humbles the exalted. He gifts the unlikely and empowers the weak. He uses those whom we might view as decidedly second-string and makes them shine like superstars, although they hardly notice. They're too busy being caught up in a story bigger than their own.

The shepherd boy whom God called as king might have been just as happy composing psalms and tending sheep and playing his harp. But God had other plans. He had a giant for David to slay (again, in a most unconventional way), armies for him to conquer, cities to save, lives to spare, men to lead and befriend, and even great sins from which to recover. David had plans, too, of what he would do for God. He dreamed of building a house for God, saying, "I dwell in a house of cedar, but the ark of God dwells in a tent" (2 Samuel 7:2, ESV). Again, God had other plans. "I took you from the pasture," He told David through the prophet Nathan,

> from following the sheep, to be ruler over My people Israel. I have been with you wherever you have gone and have cut off all your enemies from before you; and I will make you a great name, like the names of the great men who are on the earth. I will also appoint a place for My people Israel and will plant them, that they may live in their own place and not be disturbed again, nor will the wicked afflict them any more as formerly, even from the day that I commanded judges to be over My people Israel; and I will give you rest from all your enemies. The LORD also declares to you that the LORD will make a house for you. When your days are

complete and you lie down with your fathers, I will raise
up your descendant after you, who will come forth from
you, and I will establish his kingdom. He shall build a
house for My name, and I will establish the throne of his
kingdom forever.... Your house and your kingdom shall
endure before Me forever; your throne shall be established
forever. (7:8–13, 16)

God had designs on His shepherd-boy-made-king, and He has
designs on me. I may not be up front when the footlights shine, and
I may not be the woman people stand in line to see. No matter. He
can still use me for His purposes in likely and unlikely ways. Tomorrow or the next day may offer a moment in which I can be fully
present to another soul and not flinch. In which I might play against
type and be recruited to do something at which I have never ex-
celled, all for His great name and fame, and for someone else's good.

Spiritual writer Henri Nouwen calls this process *being given*. "It
is only as people who are given," he says,

that we can fully understand our being chosen, blessed, and
broken. In the giving it becomes clear that we are chosen,
blessed, and broken not simply for our own sakes, but so
that all we live finds its final significance in its being lived
for others....

Although it often seems that people give only to receive, I believe that, beyond all our desires to be appreci-
ated, rewarded, and acknowledged, there lies a simple and
pure desire to give.... Our humanity comes to its fullest
bloom in giving. We become beautiful people when we
give whatever we can give: a smile, a handshake, a kiss, an
embrace, a word of love, a present, a part of our life...all
of our life.[2]

Young David's résumé for monarchy was admittedly thin.
"Tends sheep. Composes music. Plays harp. May have killed a lion
or two to protect his flock." But God looks not on outward appearance (or padded résumé) but at the heart. Not afraid to cast
against type, He considers the young, small, inexperienced singer-
shepherd boy and whispers to Samuel: "This one. I choose him. He
is Mine."

Are you a self-employed accountant? It's not about the finan-
cial statement. A small-town carpenter? It's not about the cabinet.
A first-year teacher? It's not about the lesson plan or the test scores.
A hitless songwriter? It's not about the music. You are called to be
a player in God's great enterprise, and He cares very little for your
talent or fame, or for mine. He means for us to reincarnate "the
Word made flesh." That's our assignment. It would be a shame for
us to miss it for a show of our own making.

He must become greater; I must become less.

—JOHN 3:30, NIV

Therefore, as God's chosen people, holy and dearly loved, clothe yourselves with compassion, kindness, humility, gentleness and patience. Bear with each other and forgive whatever grievances you may have against one another. Forgive as the Lord forgave you. And over all these virtues put on love, which binds them all together in perfect unity.

—COLOSSIANS 3:12–14, NIV

One Smooth Stone

The God Who Writes on Hearts

I will give you a new heart, and a new spirit I will put
within you. And I will remove the heart of stone from
your flesh and give you a heart of flesh. And I will put
my Spirit within you, and cause you to walk in my
statutes and be careful to obey my rules.... You shall
be my people, and I will be your God.

—EZEKIEL 36:26–28, ESV

Small. Smooth. Cold. Solid. This palm-sized stone might have been plucked from a riverbed or an ancient road. It could have rested in a garden grove, or beneath a cooking fire. Nothing about one lifeless stone is extraordinary but this: Once my heart was just as lifeless. Just as cold. Just as hard. Today it beats with the steady rhythm of grace. Today, a new story is being written upon my heart by the One who gave it life, line by perfect line.

*F*our-year-old Julian arrived early for his first day of preschool, and things moved rapidly downhill from there. I encountered Julian in the hallway, where the school's social worker was trying in vain to comfort him. He wasn't just crying; he was wailing. He clutched her hand, but it provided little comfort. She spoke soothingly, but I doubted he could hear anything beyond his own sobs.

Imagining an accident of some sort, I scanned the nearby floor for blood, but whatever awful thing had just happened, it apparently wouldn't require stitches. I sidled past them and ducked into the office of the administrator I had come to see.

"Is that little guy going to be all right?" I asked her, gesturing to the hallway. She assured me that he was. My friend explained that Julian's father had dropped him off moments before and that the child was terrified that he'd been abandoned to these strangers forever! Although he was promised repeatedly that in just a few hours his dad would be back to pick him up, he wasn't buying it. Before the social worker had taken over, Julian had been sitting in the same chair I now occupied while my friend had tried to soothe him. She described to me how, when she'd asked him what was wrong, he had grabbed the front of his little shirt and gasped out these words: "My heart. It's *beating*."

She told him that his heart was supposed to beat. That a beating heart was a very good thing. That his heart had always been beating—for as far back as he could remember, and farther still. He violently shook his head no. "It never has before," he insisted.

Apparently little Julian had been living a grand total of four years yet had never felt the full weight of life—complete with fear, anxiety, heightened senses, and adrenaline—until that day. It was almost as if, on the first day of school, along with his new crayons and backpack and scissors and stickers, he'd been issued a brand-new heart. For better or worse, in a matter of moments Julian had come to experience life in a new and different way, and he would never be the same.

The prophet Ezekiel spoke to God's people in the sixth-century BC, after they had broken faith with God and been forced from their homeland. Before languishing in Babylon, these exiles had spurned God's glory in favor of the gods of the neighboring nations. They'd been unfaithful, and now they were bearing the consequences of that unfaithfulness.

But while God's people may have jilted Him, God had not jilted them. He continued to speak through the words of His prophets, both rebuking them and promising them restoration for the sake of His own holy name. Time after time they had stiff-armed their God. But even as He disciplined them for their willful disobedience, He planned to woo them back. He had claimed them as His own. He would not let them go.

"For behold, I am for you," Ezekiel said on God's behalf,

and I will turn to you, and you shall be tilled and
sown. And I will multiply people on you, the whole
house of Israel, all of it. The cities shall be inhabited
and the waste places rebuilt. And I will multiply on
you man and beast, and they shall multiply and be
fruitful. And I will cause you to be inhabited as in
your former times, and will do more good to you
than ever before. Then you will know that I am the
LORD. (Ezekiel 36:9–11, ESV)

Orphaned from their home, the children of God felt their need
for Him in a new, fresh way. That need caused them to draw close
again and listen to Ezekiel's words. But hearing was not enough.
What they needed, he told them, was a brand-new kind of heart.
Not a stone-cold, hard, unrepentant one. A tender, vulnerable,
needy heart of flesh. So God proposed a transplant: "Give Me your
heart of stone, and I will replace it with a beating heart of flesh and
blood."

Since the day God banished Adam and Eve from Eden, every heir
of theirs has been born into captivity, far from his or her true home.
Including you and me. We're dead men and dead women walking.
But then God awakens in us a desire to return home. Only our

long-lost home is not a destination on a map; it is a destination of the heart.

We belong with the God who created us. Once He dwelt among His people in a tent of meeting, and later in a temple. Today, by way of His beautiful cross, He makes His home even nearer. He comes to dwell in human hearts. But before He can inhabit a heart, He must first quicken it.

Like the exiled children of Israel, my heart once resembled a stone. Oh, it beat in my chest all right. I was breathing. But I had yet to experience the life that is truly life. With that old, hard heart I was dead in my tracks. Until God intervened. He drew me to Himself; applied the blood of His perfect Son to my heart the way the priests once applied the blood of bulls and goats and lambs to themselves, the altar, and the people; and He made me new. But He wasn't done. There was more.

Once my heart became His dwelling place, it also became His tablet to write upon in any way He wished. His story became my story, and my story became His. He would write on my heart not just law, but love. He would inscribe on me His name like a tattoo so that I would know whose I was. He would write His plans for my future and the things that are mine to do. And by His grace, I would read them, know them, and do them.

I would become a living letter written by His hand.

Paul understood this supernatural transformation, writing to his dear friends at Corinth: "You show that you are a letter from Christ delivered by us, written not with ink but with the Spirit of the living God, not on tablets of stone but on tablets of human hearts" (2 Corinthians 3:3, ESV).

What does a living letter look like? Each one is unique. But when you see a life that bears the markings of God's pen, you know it. "Once in a while," writes Frederick Buechner, we will encounter someone who "has seen him plain somehow and known him, because there are such people in the world, people whose lives flicker with the life they have seen, and whose words and lives make our scalps tingle, make us believe that there actually was a Jesus once and…still is."[1]

God's lines upon my heart can be read when I am wiser than I might be, kinder than I usually am, truer than I've ever been, more patient than I once was. They can be articulated clearly in a moment of unscripted sacrifice—when I've placed another's agenda before my own or surrendered my rights for the good of someone else. That's how I know He is making a story of my life, rewriting me from the inside out. That's how I know my heart really is beating in time with the heart of Jesus Christ.

"I have it in me," says Buechner, "to be Christ to other people. And so, of course, have we all—the life-giving, life-saving, and healing power to be saints, to be Christs, maybe at rare moments even to ourselves."[2]

The stone among God's collected treasures might just be the most precious remnant of all. It confirms what I could never reasonably hope and surely don't deserve: He loves me. I am *His* treasure. He has spared nothing in drawing me back to Himself and has placed in me a heart that can respond to His, giving Him back the love He *does* deserve. All of Him, once for all, for all of me.

And in case you're wondering, Julian's dad came back for him that first day of school—just as he promised he would. And Julian discovered that his "brand-new" beating heart was a very good thing after all.

God, being rich in mercy, because of the great love
with which he loved us, even when we were dead in
our trespasses, made us alive together with Christ.

—EPHESIANS 2:4–5, ESV

I have been crucified with Christ. It is no longer I who
live, but Christ who lives in me. And the life I now live
in the flesh I live by faith in the Son of God, who loved
me and gave himself for me.

—GALATIANS 2:20, ESV

Inside My Cigar Box

The Things That Make the Story Mine

When all the nation had finished passing over the Jordan, the LORD said to Joshua, "Take twelve men from the people, from each tribe a man, and command them, saying, 'Take twelve stones from here out of the midst of the Jordan…and bring them over with you and lay them down in the place where you lodge tonight.'"…

The people came up out of the Jordan on the tenth day of the first month, and they encamped at Gilgal on the east border of Jericho. And those twelve stones, which they took out of the Jordan, Joshua set up at Gilgal. And he said to the people of Israel, "When your children ask their fathers in times to come, 'What do these stones mean?' then you shall let your children know, 'Israel passed over this Jordan on dry ground.'"

—JOSHUA 4:1–3, 19–22, ESV

I don't have a treasure box filled with mementos of my walk with Christ. I have a *life* filled with them.

We have history, He and I—a long history that extends at least as far back as my earliest memory, maybe longer. When people ask to hear the story of how I came to know Jesus, I tell them it's not really a very dramatic one. But it is beautiful. At least to me. The simplest way to say it is that I grew up with Him. My parents believed. And their parents believed. I started attending church horizontally— lying down in the pew with my head in my mother's lap and my feet in my dad's. My chief concern back then was how to keep my shoes from falling off or my ruffled panties from showing while I napped through the sermon. (This was before children's church.)

When I got a little older, I was expected to sit upright in the pew each week…and to be quiet and still. I was allowed to hold the hymnal but not to rustle its pages. I was given my own tiny, black leather Bible with my name imprinted on it in gold. I once embellished one of its pages with my father's blue ballpoint during the Sunday-morning service and was immediately stood upright and spanked for doing so. (This was before spanking went out of fashion.) Soon after this I gave up art for good and became a writer instead. Nowadays I mark in my Bibles frequently, with no unpleasant consequences. But I do respect them. A lot.

Church was one of the most familiar places of my childhood. I knew its stairs and pews and doors and the waxy-sweet smell of polish on the wood. I knew when to sit and stand, when to speak and sing and listen. Listening proved to be good practice for almost everything in life, as it turned out. And what I heard there would change me forever. One summer a Vacation Bible School teacher pulled me aside and shared with me the simple facts of the gospel. I'd heard them before, but that day they took root in my heart for good. The "world" that "God so loved" in John 3:16 narrowed to eight-year-old me, and I believed.

That's how our story began. There have been many significant milestones along the way. I imagine them like the stones the children of Israel set up in the Jordan River, then moved to its far banks when they crossed into Canaan. The stones reminded the Israelites of what God had done on their behalf and marked their entry into the land He had promised them. The stones would help them remember to tell the story of their deliverance to their children…and to anyone else who might ask, "What do these stones mean?"

The following "Ebenezer" stones (see 1 Samuel 7:12) serve as markers to remind me of my own personal journey with God. Some of them I have actually saved. Some are long missing, held only in memory. If I had a collection of treasures representing my history with God, these would surely be found among them.

My First Bible

It is small. It fits in the palm of my hand now. The black leather cover says in all gold caps: NEW TESTAMENT, then immediately below it, PSALMS. At the very bottom edge my name is imprinted in gold caps: LEIGH MCLEROY. A tiny purple satin ribbon bisects its pages between Luke 21 and 22. The only stray mark it contains is opposite a dark and brooding illustration of the crucifixion, bearing the caption "Two thieves were crucified with Jesus." This is the mark I was spanked for making; it is smack in the middle of page 223.

This old Bible still smells like church once smelled to me. They say that smell is the sense that bears the strongest link to unconscious memory, and I believe it. I close my eyes and sniff these pages and I am *there*. It pleases me that the first object in my box is a book. Words were what He used from the very beginning to steal my heart away.

I have owned more Bibles than I can count; today no less than a dozen are shelved in my study, each acquired at a different time, for different reasons. One is in Portuguese. One I consider my college Bible. Two were gifts from publishers. Others contain various study helps. But not one of them means more to me than this one, my only King James and the oldest of them all. A small tear in the spine flies out like a tiny flag, and my name is written on the "presented to" page by me…in pencil. It is correctly spelled. A dusty worn shadow in the middle of the cover must be from my own hand—where I clutched my little Bible to carry it.

I cannot look at this first Bible without feeling a lump in my throat. I am more grateful than I can say to have been introduced to its contents so early, and to have fallen in love with its truth and beauty. I put it away with a brush down the cover and a soft kiss on the worn spot. It is sweet to me. So sweet.

A Silver Dennis the Menace Spoon

Cartoon Dennis in his striped T-shirt and coveralls smiles from the nonbusiness end of this little spoon. It was awarded to me in Sunday school in Refugio, Texas, for memorizing Bible verses. I don't recall how many verses I had to memorize to receive it—but it reminds me that my competitive streak apparently began early and helped to get the Bible out of my hand and into my head, and heart.

Back then I must have memorized the Bible verses mostly for reward. Today I know those verses by heart not because I worked to commit them to memory but because they proved so true to me that I could not keep them out. The blessing for this unintended discipline is the words themselves and nothing more—words that come rushing up from nowhere when I need them most. Words that reassure, challenge, convict, comfort, encourage, and whet my appetite for more of the great, good God I love. Words like: "I give eternal life to them, and they will never perish; and no one will snatch them out of My hand. My Father, who has given them to Me, is greater than all; and no one is able to snatch them out of the

Father's hand" (John 10:28–29, unintentionally memorized when my own father was having bypass surgery more than thirty years ago—thank You, God, for keeping him then, and for keeping me always).

A Sugar Cube with Elmer's Glue

We built a model of Jerusalem in Vacation Bible School the summer after second grade. The city walls were made of sugar cubes stacked and glued one upon another. (I'm sure a few of these bricks were also eaten in the process, hopefully before the glue was applied.) We populated our holy city with people—wooden spoons with faces drawn on them and fabric fastened around their middles with colored pipe cleaners.

I'm not sure of much more that happened that summer in VBS except for this: I deliberately put my trust in Jesus that week. I'd heard of Him all my life—of how He came to earth and lived a perfect life, then died on a cross for my sins—but before then He was only a story to me. Sometime during the week a teacher took me aside and shared John 3:16. Why she singled me out I do not know, and I don't remember her name. What I do remember is being sure—so sure—that Jesus died for *me*. That He was mine, and I was His.

I tell people now that He had to get to me young—that I

would need Him to grow up, and that I would have been far, far too hard to convince (or to convict) later on. Nothing—*nothing*—in my life compares to knowing that I belong to Him.

I hope in heaven I meet that VBS teacher and she can tell me more about that week, things I can't remember. I want to kiss her cheek and say, "Thank you. Thank you for taking me aside. Thank you for listening to the still, small voice that prompted you to do so. Thank you for building a sugar-cube Jerusalem with me and my friends when I'm sure you had plenty of other, more pressing things to do. Your obedience has meant the world to me."

A Ceramic Foal Figurine, Lying Down

I was a horse-crazy kid. More than I wanted anything else as a child, I wanted a horse. I had pictures of horses pasted up in my room and books about horses tucked away in the headboard of my twin bed. I must have read *Black Beauty* at least a dozen times. My parents never came through with the real thing (I'm sure subdivision deed restrictions had a lot to do with this), but they gave me many tokens like this one that acknowledged my passion.

I eventually put the figurines and books away and focused my attention on other things. But when I was in my thirties, I saw a movie called *The Horse Whisperer*, which had a pivotal scene that left me in a blubbering heap and opened a window into my old horse-loving days. Not long after, I went to watch a real live horse whisperer and learned a lesson in irresistible grace that I will never, ever forget.

I didn't know enough at the time to discuss effectual calling or reformed theology. I just knew that the interaction I witnessed that night between a horse named Willy and the horse whisperer who beckoned him was exactly what had happened long ago to *me*.

I still have the figurine. It has a small chip on the foal's outstretched foreleg. I like to hold it in my hand and remember how it was to be called by a God who whispers grace to the children He loves. (And I still hope one day to have the real thing.)

A Poem and Pine Needles

At twenty I was weeks away from my junior year of college…and traveling to Glorieta, New Mexico, with forty or so fellow members of the Aggie Baptist Student Union for a summer student conference. Torrential rains came midweek and caused the giant tents we camped in to collapse and our belongings to slide away in the ensuing flood. We spent the rest of our time there making do with shared clothes and sleeping on the floors of other schools' cabins. I was glad to be there but was nursing a badly broken heart. No one knew. I covered it well.

Sometime during the week my introverted nature got the better of me, and I slipped away to the prayer gardens alone with a backpack, pen and paper, and a granola bar. A trail up the mountain looked more interesting than the benches in the garden, so I began to climb. An hour or so later I was high above the property, alone in a place so quiet that all I could hear was the wind. I began to pray, then to sing, then to listen, making myself as still as I could.

Then, to quote C. S. Lewis, God came in. I cannot say more than that. He was there. I knew I was not alone. I was almost afraid that if I reached out my hand, I might touch His own hand or the hem of His robe. I took out my notebook and began to write—page after page after page, as if I were taking dictation. A key turned in my heart that day and opened it with just the gentlest little click. Then He came in.

I kept one of those hiking poems scratched on a yellowing piece of paper. In the fold of it rests a cluster of three pine needles—once soft, now brittle. These are the words on the paper:

If I hadn't been so headstrong
maybe the scars wouldn't number
quite so many.
But how can I question the way I came
when you knew all along
how often I'd have to fall before
I let someone else pick me up?
Thank you for the bruises and
the broken hearts,

the helpless tears and shattered dreams
that brought me to this hillside
and this heart-side.
Thank you for the little girl
twelve years before who said
yes to your love,
and the woman here today who can
finally take your hand
and make that "yes" forever.

It has only lately occurred to me that pine needles grow (and fall) in threes, as these did. Father, Son, and Holy Spirit—my triune God made Himself real to me as I perched on a rock, under a cloudy New Mexico sky.

A Glass Box Filled with Ashes

How best to dispose of a dream? And if that dream has become something of a stubborn idol, shouldn't it be done in a way that precludes reconstitution? This small glass container served as a reminder of the evening, alone in my apartment, when I burned a stack of journal pages in the fireplace and said good-bye to a recurring dream. I let it go, believing that God could resurrect it if He chose, or pull me past it for the better.

After I watched the pages burn to black feathery bits, I knelt on my sofa and looked out my window at the sky. The moon that night was as full and round and luminous as I had ever seen it. It seemed to hang low enough to rest on the roof of a nearby building. It looked for all the world like a promise to me: *I will make your heart whole. Trust Me. I will do it for you.*

I believe Him. And I'm holding Him to that promise. The box and the ashes are long gone, and so is the particular possibility they represented. But the promise of that beautiful moon, well, it remains. I've been told that only time—and turning—makes the half moon whole.

My Jesus Card

My faith upbringing was very nearly tokenless. Southern Baptists don't have much in the way of holy bits, as some religions do. For two of my childhood years, we lived next-door to a big, loving Catholic family, and one of their six children was my best friend. (He remembered years later that I had told him—at age seven—that he couldn't be my boyfriend because I already had one. I had to ask if he recalled who I'd said it was!) He and I rode our bikes together, made tents in the backyard, and went to and from school in each other's company. One summer our parents allowed each of us to attend the other's summer church activities; I went with Jackie to something called CCD, and he came with me to Vacation Bible School. At the end of our trading-places week, I decided that his church had the best stuff. They had holy cards and incense, candles, guitars, wine, and rosaries. We mostly had crayons, felt boards, and punch.

Years later I was teaching an adult Bible-study class, and for some reason I mentioned this in the course of the lesson. Afterward a girl I'd never met came up to me and quietly pressed something into my hand. "It's a holy card," she whispered. "I want you to have it." I have carried it ever since.

My holy card has Jesus on the front, so I've named it my "Jesus card." He looks absolutely invincible, rising white robed from the tomb while Roman guards and angels quiver at His feet. Light pours from the wounds in His hands and side, and a halo rings His head. On the back of the card are printed these words: JESUS, HELP ME! The prayer that follows calls on Jesus to do just that, saying, "In every need let me come to You with humble trust, saying: Jesus, help me!" Not a bad prayer, when you think of it.

My Jesus card suggests that I might ask for His help "in all my doubts, perplexities, and temptations; in hours of loneliness, weariness, and trials; when my heart is cast down at failure, seeing no good come from my efforts; and in the failure of my plans and hopes, in disappointments, troubles, and sorrows."

My friends sometimes laugh when I pull out my Jesus card,

but it reminds me that He is, and has always been, my best hope in any test or trial. It has been good for me to learn to say, in spite of my tendency toward pride and self-sufficiency, "Jesus, help me!"

A Broken Piece of Slate
(from Oswald Chambers's Roof)

Sometime during my college years I was given a copy of Oswald Chambers's *My Utmost for His Highest*. This classic devotional has been a faithful companion for almost three decades now. It never gets old to me. I have plowed through three different copies of the book, giving two away and wearing one completely out.

Oswald Chambers was a Scotsman converted under the ministry of Charles Spurgeon. He studied architecture at the University of Edinburgh, then theology at Dunoon College. In the early 1900s Chambers was an itinerant Bible teacher at home and abroad; then in 1915 he sailed to Egypt, where he served as a YMCA chaplain during World War I. A short time later at the age of forty-three, he died of a ruptured appendix.

Chambers never saw the book that bears his name. His wife—a trained stenographer—had taken notes at nearly every lecture he ever gave. She had them published after his death as *My Utmost*, and the book has been in print ever since.

After spending several days in Oxford, England, one summer

working on the restoration of The Kilns (the former home of C. S. Lewis), I met a friend in Scotland, where we rented a car and traveled several more days. We both wanted to see Dunoon, and there we were directed to the school where Chambers studied and spoke. It had become a bed-and-breakfast, but in recent days a fire had closed it down. When my friend and I arrived, the building was abandoned. We walked around it, peeking inside at charred remains. As we were leaving, I bent down and picked up a piece of slate from the ground, probably from the building's roof. I placed it in my copy of *My Utmost,* alongside a sprig of heather.

Chambers died decades before I was born, but we are connected, he and I. His words have been touchstones at countless points in my life. I haven't just read his book—I've argued with it, grieved over it, wrestled with it, and been soundly challenged by it. I've written in its margins year after year and quoted it so often I should pay royalties to his heirs. Two particular phrases will stay with me until I die: "You can never sanctify to God that with which you long to satisfy yourself"[1] and "The one true mark of a saint of God is the inner creativity that flows from being totally surrendered to Jesus Christ."[2] Both are written on my heart as surely as if they were tattooed there.

To see the place where Chambers no doubt spoke some of the words I have treasured made me glad. And the piece of slate reminds me that my own words may outlive me…and that I should choose them prayerfully and use them sparingly, concerned not for my own legacy but for His glory alone.

A Photograph of Circle Bluff,
near Leakey, Texas

You can see the bend in the river in this shot, and the leaves on the trees below are dressed in fall colors. A rock ledge juts into the picture's foreground, and my feet dangle off of it, clad in sturdy brown hiking boots. This place is called Circle Bluff, and from its vantage point I am perched high above the Frio River, on the H. E. Butt Foundation property near Leakey, Texas. It is one of my favorite places on the planet.

I began coming to the canyon in 1992, to a small cottage called the Quiet House—a place built for personal prayer and contemplation. If it is possible to have a long-term relationship with a place on a map, I have one with this place. Year after year, trip after trip, I drive through the rock entrance, wind down a gravel road into the canyon, drive through the river to a tiny three-room rock house, and begin to breathe more deeply than I did just moments before. In this blessed place, my heart knows what to do. Each time I go, it feels like stealing away to meet a lover—and in the truest sense, I am.

Years' worth of journals in the house chronicle cross sections of the lives of wayfarers who have stayed within its walls; a handful of these entries are in my own handwriting. We are connected, all of us, to one another and to this place—drawn together by a sacred cord of belief. We do not just believe in God; we believe that He might meet us here. And He does.

Each time I go (if the weather permits) I hike the well-marked trails of the camp, winding down and around the beautiful canyon to the river, and finally climbing up high above it. In the course of these hikes I have seen deer and wild turkeys, raccoons, skunks, wild javelinas—and once a bobcat that seemed to follow me for many yards, then lose interest in my scent. I'm a city girl, but I've never been afraid in this place. I am held here.

I've come here to write, to pray, to rest, to relinquish, to ask, to remember, and to dream. If I had only a few days left on earth—and knew it—I would want to come here one more time. This place seems not so very far from heaven, after all. Perhaps the bluff I must climb is the footstool where the King of Glory rests His feet. I am thankful just to sense His nearness in the cedar-scented canyon air.

A Page from the Hymnal

This one, hymn number two, is titled "Love Divine, All Loves Excelling." The particular page is no longer attached to its source: an old Baptist Hymnal from the First Baptist Church of Ballinger, Texas. I do not know how the hymnal came to be in my possession, but Ballinger is the tiny West Texas town in which my mother grew up—the town where both of her parents lived, died, and were buried. My grandmother once lived right across the street from the Baptist Church; I believe my parents were married in the pastor's study.

Hymn number two was written by Charles Wesley, and I know each word of it by heart. Hymns were the music of my childhood; my theology, I suspect, was shaped as much by them as it was by the Word proclaimed from the pulpit on any given Sunday.

Many of the choruses and worship songs favored today seem less instructive, both poetically and spiritually. As a child, I pondered phrases from hymns like "Lord, let me never, never outlive my love for Thee" from "O Sacred Head, Now Wounded," wondering, what would *that* be like? Or singing, "Let Thy goodness, like a fetter, bind my wandering heart to Thee" from "Come, Thou Fount of Every Blessing" and asking first, "What's a fetter?" then, "Why is it goodness that might bind my heart to God?" I love those words. They've given me something over time that I can't imagine getting any other way.

It is sad to me that very few children today will share my experience, not only of hearing great hymns sung week after week, but of repeatedly hearing truths that were way, way over my head. Not only did these songs challenge my thinking; they connected me in ways I probably still cannot entirely grasp to the great "cloud of witnesses" who sang them before me. That number includes my parents, their parents, and even the great-grandparents I never knew.

I've heard hymns that I've long known sung in Spanish, in Portuguese, and even in Romanian. They seem to transcend not just time but also culture and circumstance, drawing us together as one church, one body. When I hear them in unfamiliar languages and dialects, it is not hard to imagine a day when we will be "changed from glory into glory, till in heaven we take our place, till we cast our crowns before Thee, lost in wonder, love, and praise."[3]

A Brittle, Heart-Shaped Leaf

Forty-something women who have never married have a not-so-secret tendency to loathe Valentine's Day. Depending on the circumstances, I can share that tendency. On this particular February 14, I was feeling left out, unloved, and forgotten. Not just by Mr. Wonderful, wherever he might be, but even, a little, by God. How could He have overlooked for so long the simple desire of my heart to belong to someone?

Believing that getting a move on is better than sulking, I clipped my dog's leash to his collar, and we set out on a walk through our neighborhood. I had not gone a dozen feet from my front door when I saw on the sidewalk a perfect, heart-shaped leaf—only this leaf was not green. It was brown and worn so paper thin by rain and sun and wind that it looked like lace. It seemed so fragile I was almost afraid to pick it up—but that would have been like refusing to open an envelope addressed to me. This leaf was mine. My own odd valentine, delivered to my doorstep by the very breath of God.

This heart said that God is nearer than my thoughts and that nothing in my own heart is hidden from Him. That He knows my desires, even the silent ones, and He takes notice of them. Its tissue-thin state was a reminder of my own heart's vulnerability and an encouragement to entrust it first to the One who knows it best. And even though this leaf looked past its prime, its edges were perfect, and it was indeed beautiful.

For reasons I cannot explain, God has kept me—at least this far—entirely to Himself. But He has kept me perfectly, and with a fragile beauty that simply cannot fade. With one well-timed leaf He whispered, *I have loved you with an everlasting love.* And so He has.

A Handful of Feathers

These delicate calling cards of nature are a symbol of hope to me, because of Emily Dickinson's perfectly true "'Hope' is the thing with feathers…"

I've saved a few of these feathers I've found—either because they came at a time when I was desperately in need of a little hope or because they were found in an unusual place or just because they were oddly beautiful to me. These feathers are a little wink from God that says, *I hold your hopes, and I haven't forgotten.* They remind me to be on the lookout for His goodness and mercy everywhere and to keep looking for it until I see it clearly.

There is so much glory and wonder in this world, if we will only notice it. So much intricate beauty and so many details worth reveling in. "God invades our world often. He invades *my* world often. And I'm afraid I miss too many of those moments because I'm simply not expecting them. I don't look for them. I don't listen, and watch, and hope to hear his voice in whatever way he chooses to speak."[4] But the feathers remind me that I should.

"I wait for the LORD, my soul does wait, and in His word do I hope," writes the psalmist. "My soul waits for the Lord more than the watchmen for the morning; indeed, more than the watchmen for the morning. O Israel, hope in the LORD, for with the LORD there is lovingkindness, and with Him is abundant redemption" (Psalm 130:5–7).

Will you wait and hope and watch too?

One day He will change us—and this beautiful but broken world in which we live—into something new and shining and glorious. Until then, we groan for what we wish we were but are not, wish we had but do not, wish we might see but cannot. But He is with us, even now. We do not wait in vain.

One day we will exchange our small box of treasures for His infinite one, and it will take forever to see what He has saved.

You have multiplied, O LORD my God,

your wondrous deeds and your thoughts toward us;

none can compare with you!

I will proclaim and tell of them,

yet they are more than can be told.

—PSALM 40:5, ESV

What's in Your Box?

Personal Reflection and Group Discussion Guide

*C*losing the cover of a book can feel like saying good-bye to a dear friend. I hope that as you've read *Treasured,* you've felt yourself drawn closer to the God whose artifacts and character we've examined together—and that you are hungry to experience still more of Him. The chapters of this book could not begin to exhaust His treasures or to fully tell His story.

So why not continue the theme of *Treasured* by assembling some memories of your own? What mementos or treasures tell the story of *your* relationship with God? How have they become a part of your shared history? And how will you collect them to be cherished as evidence of God's active presence in your life on those days when you need a reminder of His goodness and grace?

You may want to consider starting a journal of your remembrances, creating a scrapbook or bulletin board highlighting treasured moments, or gathering tangible souvenirs in a small box. Whatever method or combination of methods you may choose for collecting these things, prepare for a faith-building adventure that is uniquely personal and focused. Consider God's story. Consider your story. And consider the one-of-a-kind story that is birthed when the two become intertwined.

I also invite you to share a few of your collected treasures at www.leighmcleroy.com, on the What's in Your Box? blog.

The God Who Covers Me

Adam and Eve made garments of fig leaves in an attempt to cover their sin and shame. Later God replaced those with more durable animal skins—and later still with something both perfect and permanent: the blood of His Son, Jesus (see Hebrews 9:11–14; 10:16–18).

- Think back to where and when you first received forgiveness and became "covered" and clean in Christ. Who was present with you? What was the setting? What artifact or keepsake reminds you of God's covering for your sin?
- What are some things you've used to conceal your shortcomings, and how has God replaced those fig leaves?
- On a new piece of stationery, write a thank-you note to God for His sin-covering work on your behalf.

The God of New Beginnings

Paul writes in 2 Corinthians 5:17 that "if anyone is in Christ, he is a new creation. The old has passed away; behold, the new has come" (ESV). Too often we cling to the old and shun the new, fearing change instead of embracing it. One thing is sure: in every new place or situation to which we are called, God has already gone before us.

- Can you pinpoint on a map a physical place where you once started over again? Or do you have photographs of, or letters from, someone who has been instrumental in your spiritual history?
- What is your favorite brand-new thing? (I loved brand-new crayons as a child. It was hard to begin using them!)
- In what area of life are you making a new beginning now? What tangible marker could you establish to signify this fresh start?

The God Who Sees

Is there anyone alive who hasn't felt invisible? When it seems the world has forgotten us, we might imagine that God has too. But nothing could be further from the truth.

- Describe a time when you felt invisible.
- Read Psalm 139:1–16, and copy down the phrase from David's psalm that means the most to you.

- Think back to a circumstance in which you believe God actively intervened to assure you of His presence and care. What memento—maybe an old pair of eyeglasses, a magnifying glass, or a kaleidoscope—could serve as your reminder of the God who sees?

The God Who Provides

It's hard to imagine a God who would ask a man to sacrifice his only son—especially a son whom God Himself had promised. After all, as I wrote earlier, it is a far, far easier thing to believe God's good intentions toward you when you're holding Isaac's hand in yours.

- Describe a time when you were called to sacrifice something dear to you in order to follow God more closely. What did you gain in the end?
- What object reminds you of the time and place of that sacrifice?
- Read Romans 5:6–8. Why should we believe that God will provide what we need most?

The God with a Bigger Plan

Life is not always fair. Bad things happen to good people (and to not-so-good people too). When life does not go the way we've planned—especially when others seem intent on hampering our progress—we can be confident that God's plan is bigger than ours.

- Can you recall a painful setback that turned out to be a blessing for you?
- If your life were a piece of fabric, what colors and patterns might be woven through it?
- If you are experiencing a setback now, what could you carry with you as a reminder that your story is not over yet, that God is still at work?

The God Who Defeats Death

In Psalm 23, King David writes of walking "through the valley of the shadow of death" (verse 4). But David was not afraid. The rod and staff of his Shepherd-God were a comfort to him when death drew near.

- What frightens you most about death? What comforts you?
- Jesus said, "I am the resurrection and the life; he who believes in Me will live even if he dies, and everyone who lives and believes in Me will never die" (John 11:25–26). What difference does this reassurance make when you face difficult seasons of life?
- What everyday, ordinary things remind you of the resurrection and God's power over death?

The God of Show and Tell

God cares about the details. His presence is as evident in a milk-weed plant as it is in the Milky Way. He inhabits every intersection of heaven and earth—and there are many. Where have you seen Him lately?

- We often take note of God's handiwork on the grand scale of the night sky or a gorgeous sunrise, but what is your favorite smaller-than-a-breadbox sign of His careful attention to detail?

- What token might remind you of God's presence in His created world? A postcard from the Grand Canyon? An aspen leaf? A ticket stub from an aquarium, planetarium, or flower show? Something else?

- First Peter 2:9 says, "You are a chosen people, a royal priesthood, a holy nation, a people belonging to God, that you may declare the praises of him who called you out of darkness into his wonderful light" (NIV). Where could you declare His praises today, and to whom?

The God Who Includes

Have you ever been picked last for softball? passed over for a promotion you believed you deserved? left alone on the edge of a dance floor, hoping to be asked to take a spin? Then you know firsthand how it feels to be excluded. What about the reverse? Have you ever excluded someone else because you considered the person different, awkward, or unlovely?

- Read Isaiah 53:3. Who might best understand the misunderstood or the excluded? Why?
- Do you consider yourself an outsider or an insider in God's family? Why?
- Make a "reminder in red" to represent Rahab and God's penchant for including the most unlikely characters in His story.

The God Who Speaks

We think of prayer as an exercise in speaking, but listening should be an active part of our prayers as well. How long has it been since you set aside time to listen for God's voice?

- Read Psalms 61 and 62. One is a cry for God to listen; the other declares the psalmist's intent to listen to God. Which psalm resembles most of your prayers?
- Practice listening. Spend an hour without speaking, and record every sound you hear. What did you learn by being silent?
- Has a special piece of music moved you? Place a copy of the lyrics or a recording of the song in your collection.

The God Who Gleans Joy from Sorrow

Plots are driven, good storytellers say, by conflict. In Naomi's story, she is beset by the sorrow of losing her husband and both of her sons. Those losses were defining events in her life. They were also events that generations later led to the birth of Jesus of Nazareth in Bethlehem. "He heals the brokenhearted," says the psalmist, "and binds up their wounds. He determines the number of the stars; he gives to all of them their names. Great is our Lord, and abundant in power; his understanding is beyond measure" (Psalm 147:3–5, ESV).

- Take a blank card, and on one side write a "before" word or phrase to describe yourself at your worst. On the other side write a word or phrase to describe yourself after God intervened on your behalf. (For example, Naomi's card might have read "bitter widow," then "blessed grandmother.")

- What was your favorite story as a child? What did you love most about that story? Do you still have a copy of it? If so, read it again. How is it like your own story? How is it different?

- What would you consider a defining moment of your life? Can you see in retrospect how God was present in your time of testing?

The God of the Little Guy

The Bible is full of characters that are cast against type. Moses, a murderer who didn't speak so well, became the one who delivered his people from slavery. Abraham, an old, childless man with an infertile wife, became the father of Israel. David, a young music-obsessed boy with a cast of older, more qualified brothers, became the king of Israel.

- Name a time when you felt miscast or ill equipped for the task before you. Did you question whether God was right about you, or did you trust His plan?
- The acorn that grows into a towering oak tree, the mustard seed that produces a huge bush—what other small items hold great potential?
- Mother Teresa said, "In this life we cannot do great things. We can only do small things with great love." What small thing could you do today with great love?

The God Who Writes on Hearts

God's desire to write on the hearts of His people demonstrates His desire to come close and live intimately with them. He says, "I will put My Spirit within them" (see Ezekiel 11:19). Imagine: the Spirit of God not just near or next to us—but inside us!

- Read John 16:1–15. What does Jesus say the Holy Spirit will come to do?

- How responsive are you to the things God writes on your heart? Do you ignore Him, try to second-guess Him, or trust Him and believe what He says about you is true?

- Start a rock collection! Gather some small, smooth stones and write promises from God's Word on them, then display them in a way that reminds you often of what He can do. Why not start with "I have called you by name; you are Mine!" (Isaiah 43:1).

Acknowledgments

Book writing is a solitary task, but book birthing involves an army. I am deeply grateful for the fellowship and expertise of the friends and colleagues who helped bring this particular book to life. For kind hospitality in the days prior to my deadline (after being made temporarily homeless by a fire), thank you, Jeannene, Allyson and Walter, Marcy and Rick, and Flo and Jim. You didn't just give me shelter; you made me feel at home.

Thank you, Howard Butt and the staff of Laity Lodge, for ten well-timed days of solitude and undistracted focus in the Frio River Canyon. Only heaven will tell how many good things have been born in the stillness of that place. To praying friends Barney and Karen, Carlos and Sandra, and Steve and Karen; to Monday-nighters Erin, Rachel, Anke, Juli, Robyn, Julie, Jane, Sandra, and Jen; and to my City of Refuge family—you're simply the best. Lynn, Mom, and Dad—we're in it for life. I love you.

Thanks to Jeanette, who "got" this book early on, and to Lee, who shaped, shopped, and sold it with wisdom and integrity. Thank you, Laura, for your keen eye and gently rendered edits.

Thank you, reader, for opening this cover to begin. I wrote with you in mind.

Ever since I was young, I've saved the best for last. Thank You, Jesus, for making much of my little faith and for loving me so well. You are mine, and I am ever Yours.

Notes

Chapter 1

1. G. K. Chesterton, *Orthodoxy* (London: John Lane, 1909), 22.

2. John Piper, "Battling the Unbelief of Misplaced Shame," sermon, October 2, 1988, www.desiringgod.org/Resource Library/Sermons/ByDate/1988/653_Battling_the _Unbelief_of_Misplaced_Shame.

Chapter 2

1. T. S. Eliot, "Little Gidding," in *Four Quartets* (New York: Harcourt, 1943), 59.

2. Frederick Buechner, *The Hungering Dark* (San Francisco: HarperSanFrancisco, 1985), 41.

3. Buechner, *The Hungering Dark,* 43.

Chapter 3

1. Carolyn Custis James, *Lost Women of the Bible: Finding Strength and Significance Through Their Stories* (Grand Rapids: Zondervan, 2005), 86–87.

2. James, *Lost Women of the Bible,* 93, 98.

3. James, *Lost Women of the Bible,* 97.

4. Eugene H. Peterson, *Five Smooth Stones for Pastoral Work* (Grand Rapids: Eerdmans, 1992), 107.

5. Written in Lewis's copy of *Eternal Life* by Frederick von Hugel (in the Wade Center at Wheaton College, Wheaton, Illinois), quoted in Corbin Scott Carnell, *Bright Shadow of Reality: Spiritual Longing in C. S. Lewis* (Grand Rapids: Eerdmans, 1999), 163.

Chapter 4

1. William Shakespeare, *Henry V,* act 5, scene 2, line 3178, www.opensourceshakespeare.org.

2. Emily Dickinson, *Acts of Light,* ed. Robin Bledsoe, paintings by Nancy Ekholm Burkert (Boston: New York Graphic Society, 1980), 143.

3. C. S. Lewis, *The Weight of Glory and Other Addresses* (San Francisco: HarperSanFrancisco, 2001), 190.

4. Søren Kierkegaard, *Fear and Trembling* and *The Sickness Unto Death,* trans. Walter Lowrie (Princeton: Princeton University Press, 1953), 36.

Chapter 5

1. Emily Dickinson, *Collected Poems* (Philadelphia: Running Press, 1991), 89, emphasis added.

Chapter 6

1. John Piper, "Dying for the Glory of Christ," sermon, November 3, 2004, www.desiringgod.org/Resource Library/TasteAndSee/ByDate/2004/1273_Dying_for_ the_Glory_of_Christ.

2. Piper, "Dying for the Glory of Christ."

3. J. K. Rowling, *Harry Potter and the Deathly Hallows* (Great Britain: Bloomsbury, 2007), 554.

4. Rowling, *Harry Potter and the Deathly Hallows,* 561.

5. Rowling, *Harry Potter and the Deathly Hallows,* 561.

6. Rowling, *Harry Potter and the Deathly Hallows,* 567.

7. Rowling, *Harry Potter and the Deathly Hallows,* 268.

8. Frederick Buechner, *Godric* (New York: Atheneum, 1980), 96.

Chapter 7

1. John Wesley, "Exodus," *Explanatory Notes Upon the Old Testament,* www.christnotes.org/commentary.php?com=wes &b=2&c=39.

Chapter 8

1. Derek Webb, "A King and a Kingdom," *Mockingbird* (INO Records, 2005).

2. John Piper, "The Reformed Faith and Racial Harmony," sermon, January 19, 2003, www.desiringgod.org/

ResourceLibrary/Sermons/ByDate/2003/121_The
_Reformed_Faith_and_Racial_Harmony.

3. David A. Anderson, *Gracism: The Art of Inclusion* (Downers Grove, IL: InterVarsity, 2007), 107.

Chapter 9

1. Dallas Willard, *In Search of Guidance: Developing a Conversational Relationship with God* (Ventura, CA: Regal, 1983), 149.

2. Frederick Buechner, *Peculiar Treasures: A Biblical Who's Who* (San Francisco: Harper & Row, 1979), 13.

3. Ken Gire, *The Reflective Life: Becoming More Spiritually Sensitive to the Everyday Moments of Life* (Colorado Springs: Cook, 1998), 184.

4. Michael Card, "The Final Word," *The Final Word* (Sparrow Records, 1987).

5. Leigh McLeroy, *The Sacred Ordinary: Embracing the Holy in the Everyday* (Grand Rapids: Revell, 2008), 208.

Chapter 10

1. John Piper, "Ruth: Sweet and Bitter Providence," sermon at Bethlehem Baptist Church, July 1, 1984, www.sound ofgrace.com/piper84/070184m.htm.

2. Robert McKee, *Story: Substance, Structure, Style, and the Principles of Screenwriting* (New York: HarperCollins, 1997), 210.

3. John Piper, "Ruth: Strategic Righteousness," sermon, July 15, 1984, www.desiringgod.org/ResourceLibrary/Sermons /BySeries/57/447_Ruth_Strategic_Righteousness/.

Chapter 11

1. Eugene H. Peterson, "What Are Writers Good For?" lecture, Tattered Cover Bookstore, Denver, CO, July 9, 2006, www.alivecom.com/media/Peterson%20Lecture%20WHA T%20ARE%20WRITERS%20FOR.pdf.

2. Henri J. M. Nouwen, *Life of the Beloved: Spiritual Living in a Secular World* (New York: Crossroad, 1992), 105, 106.

Chapter 12

1. Frederick Buechner, *A Room Called Remember: Uncollected Pieces* (San Francisco: HarperSanFrancisco, 1984), 97.

2. Frederick Buechner, *Secrets in the Dark: A Life in Sermons* (San Francisco: HarperSanFrancisco, 2006), 236.

Chapter 13

1. Oswald Chambers, "The Waters of Satisfaction Scattered," in *My Utmost for His Highest* (New York: Dodd, Mead, 1935), September 3.

2. Oswald Chambers, *My Utmost for His Highest* (Grand Rapids: Discovery, 1992), June 13.

3. Charles Wesley and John Zundel, "Love Divine, All Loves Excelling," *Baptist Hymnal* (Nashville: Convention Press, 1956), 2.

4. Leigh McLeroy, *The Sacred Ordinary: Embracing the Holy in the Everyday* (Grand Rapids: Revell, 2008), 119.